Methuen Playscripts

The Methuen Playscripts series exists to extend the range of plays in print by publishing work which is not yet widely known but which has already earned a place in the acting repertoire of the modern theatre.

Sweet Talk

SWEET TALK is Michael Abbensetts's first full-length play, for which he was named joint winner of the Royal Court's 1972 George Devine Award. Set in the one-roomed 'home' of a young West Indian couple, the play deals with the problems of a faltering marriage - problems caused no less by the pressures from outside than by the strains inherent in the marriage. Michael Abbensetts writes lyrically and humorously to create a deeply moving play.

'I thought highly of Michael Abbensetts' debut, *Sweet Talk*, at the Theatre Upstairs. It's a quiet, downbeat play that comes to grips with the daily struggle to keep one's head above water in the face of an oblivious world. Without once raising his voice, the author shows us a married couple drifting inexorably into deep water and it's unnervingly real.'
W. Stephen Gilbert, *Plays and Players*

I0659425

SWEET TALK

MICHAEL ABBENSETTS

First published in Great Britain in 1974
by Eyre Methuen Ltd
11 New Fetter Lane London EC4P 4EE
Copyright © 1974 by Michael Abbensetts

Set by Expression Typesetters
Printed in Great Britain by
Fletcher & Son Ltd, Norwich

ISBN 0 413 31460 X (hardback)
ISBN 0 413 31470 7 (paperback)

To my parents

Sweet Talk was first presented by the Theatre Upstairs at the Royal Court Theatre on July 31st 1973 with the following cast:

RITA FLETCHER	Mona Hammond
TONY FLETCHER	Allister Bain
DENNIS	Don Warrington
SANDRA	Sally Watts
YVONNE	Joan-Ann Maynard
OSCAR	Lee Davis

Directed by Stephen Frears
Designed by William Dudley

The FLETCHERS' room in Shepherd's Bush - spring and summer.

ACT ONE

Scene One

House in Shepherd's Bush. The FLETCHERS' room. Spring. Evening.

RITA FLETCHER is changing her dress; she is in her petticoat. She puts on her dressing-gown. She seems very tired; she is dropping on her feet. RITA is West Indian, about twenty-five, pretty enough, takes a pride in her appearance. She crosses to bed, pumps up the pillows. The radiogram is on: an Isaac Hayes LP.

RITA gets on top of the bed, adopting a sitting-up position with the help of the pillows. She stifles a yawn. Her head sinks lower and lower.

The room is not quite the size of a double room. It is an attractive enough place. However, it is not large enough for the FLETCHERS and all their possessions. All three FLETCHERS live in this room, RITA, her husband, TONY, and BINKIE, their five year old son. TONY also has his work-bench in this room. Here at nights he builds and repairs radios and record-players and television sets. BINKIE's bed is a foldaway affair; presently it is closed up in the interests of space. A number of photographs around the room. A settee; a glass-top table (their dining table); a TV set; a radiogram and also a tape recorder. A defective paraffin heater. A few toys. What else? A child's xylophone, not a toy it plays.

On TONY's work-bench: the guts or motor of a record-player (he has just begun building a new stereo set); an old radio; voltmeter, soldering iron, transistors, etc.

TONY FLETCHER lets himself into the room. He is twenty-eight, West Indian; a very raffish looking young man. He is wearing a dark suit and an overcoat but no tie. Plus a Russian styled fur hat. He has been over in England longer than his wife has, so he has less of a West Indian accent than she has.

TONY contemplates his wife for a moment or two, none too pleased. He sucks his teeth.

He crosses to radiogram.

TONY: You want this on, woman?

    (RITA wakes, slight start.)

RITA: I din' even hear you come in.

    (TONY turns off radiogram.)

TONY (a bit satirical, but not unkindly): You din' hear me come in, oh, Loopy Loo, eh? I mighta been a rapist, Loopy Loo.

    (Sly.)

A *white* rapist.

(Boyishly.)

A sex-maniac from the Home Off-iss. Keepin' an eye on immigrants! An' not jus' an eye, neither.

(Pause.)

RITA: You finish?

TONY (grinning): I've only just come in. You ain' heard nothin' yet.

RITA (dismissing him with a wave of her hand): It's so *cold*. They call this Spring.

TONY: It's no wonder I always rush home. I like the way you leap outuh bed as soon as I get in.

(He takes off his overcoat, moves to hang it up behind the door. He still has his hat on.)

RITA (coolly): I'm tired. You know how hard I gotta work. You know that. So what're you playin' at?

(Pause.)

You think I jus' lie here 'cos I'm under contract to keep this bed company?

(Pause.)

TONY: Where's Binkie?

(Moving over to her.)

Give us a kiss, Loops.

RITA: I done kiss no man wit' a hat on.

(Pause.)

TONY (stung): Everytime I come home, you in bed!

RITA (mischievously): Correction: I'm lyin' on *topuh* the bed. They got some law that says I can't lie on topuh the bed . . . ! Since when?

(Pause.)

TONY: All women mad as hell. White or black.

(He turns away. He hangs his hat up behind the door as well. He remains in his jacket for warmth.)

RITA: I hope you realise the Tee Vee still not workin'. You mend other people's sets but not y'own.

(Pause.)

What I got to stay awake for? To watch the radiogram?

(Pause.)

You listenin' to me, boy?

(TONY gets out another pair of shoes. Pause.)

When you goin' to fix it, Tony?

(TONY sits on edge of bed, changing his shoes, his back to her.)

TONY: When you get outuh bed.

(Pause. She gets off the bed. Steps loftily over to settee. Sits herself down. Pause. TONY massages his foot.)

RITA: Well . . . ?

(Pause.)

TONY: Done bother me.

RITA: What's wrong wit' y'foot?

(Mischievously.)

I thought it was y'*mouth* you never gave a rest I never knew it was y'foot as well.

(Pause.)

TONY (his sarcasm is more playful than anything): Ow, Loopy Loo, you too sweet. Sittin' there in y'dressin'-gown. Nice. Too nice. You look - beau-ti-ful. Especially as it's not even seven o'clock yet.

(Pause.)

You goin' out. Loopy Loo? Is that why you dress up in y'Sunday best. Eh? Answer me, Loopy. Where you off to? Buckingham Pal-iss? They givin' a party? A-come-as-you-are-party. A pyjama party?

(RITA looks heavenwards, sucking her teeth.)

TONY (moving towards her): Loopy Loo, you done wanna know, right? Eh? Eh?

(Pause. Giving her a playful dig.)

I'm talkin' to you, Loopy Loo.

(She fends him off.)

RITA (patiently, as if she were dealing with an overgrown child): Tony Fletcher, stop being such an ass.

(Pause. TONY moves away. He can be quite vulnerable, sometimes.)

TONY (not looking at her): The manager called me in her office today. I got another raise. Jus' a poun'. It's better than nothing, but she always gotta act like she's givin' me the keys to Fort Knox.

(Pause.)

Still she likes me.

(Pause.)

She tole me, 'I knew you'd make a good chargehan', Tony'.

(Pause.)

Anyway, I asked her what made her say that.

(Sad smile.)

An' you know what she said, Loopy Loo? "Cos I know you, Tony!"

(Pause. Wan.)

Pretty funny, eh, Loops? She feel she know me.

(Pause.)

Yeah. Pretty funny.

(Pause. He sits at work-bench. Pause.)

RITA (gentle for her): You want y'dinner?

(Pause.)

TONY: This room . . . this room.

(Not loudly.)

Chrise, man . . . Christ.

(Pause.)

We never had it so good. Right?

(A grimace.)

Right, Loopy Loo?

(Pause. Then about paraffin heater.)

It's no wonder this room always chilly, chilly. That thing's useless.

(Sudden laugh.)

One day that heater boun' to freeze to death. Catch pneumonia! As a heater it would make a better fridge.

(He laughs some more. Stops. Then laughs to himself, boyishly.)

It'll catch a cold an' die one day.

(Pause.)

Well, let's get some work done aroun' here.

(He picks up the old radio. Sucks his teeth.)

Look at this. Just look at this . . . ! Frank call this a radio, I call it crap.

(Pause.)

Even Marconi would call it crap!

(Pause.)

He should take this somewhere else.

(Laughter.)

Like a junkyard! Or the neares' *ocean*.

(He finally runs down. Pause.)

Yeah. Very funny. Coloured people always laughin'. It's better than havin' an ace up y'sleeve, I suppose.

(Pause.)

Yeah.

(Pause. Facing RITA.)

You know there's this girl . . . an African . . . she works under me . . . today she got fired. Not becauseuh me. I din' tell them to get riduh the girl. Anyway, anyway, she got her cards.

(Pause.)

An' you know what she do? You know what that African girl do? She got down on her knees in the manager office . . . her *knees* . . . an' she beg fo' her job back. Boy, how that girl beg them an' beg them.

(Pause.)

RITA: She get her job back?

TONY: Get what job back? You think it's a fairy story I'm tellin' you?! A Hans Christian Andersen story. Where everything always ends happy ever after . . . ! Wake up, Loopy Loo.

(Pause.)

RITA: Poor girl.

TONY: Yeah.

(Almost to himself.)

We never had it so good.

(Pause. He puts the old radio aside. Lifts guts of record-player in front of him.)

This is goin' to be the best thing I ever built, Rita.

RITA (sleepily): Good, that's good, Tony.

TONY: I should be able to sell it fo' about a hundred quid. At *least*. When I finish wit' it you couldn't buy one like it in any shop fo' under two hundred. I guarantee that!

(Pause.)

You think I'm boastin', Sweet Pea?

RITA: Eh? Oh. No. You're good at y'job. I only wish I could make you see jus' how good. Maybe then you wouldn't feel so *frus-trated*.

(She has got up intending to put on another record. She has to stop; dizziness, something.)

TONY (irritated): What's the matter wit' you?

RITA: I feel a bit . . . outuh sorts, that's all.

TONY: Done look at me. I only repair record-players.

(Pause.)

RITA (quietly): It's never much use turnin' to you fo' help, right?

(Pause.)

TONY (loss, something): It was supposed to be a joke.

(Pause.)

You've not been well at all recently. You better see the doctor.

RITA (grimacing): I'll be OK.

(Pause.)

TONY: If you're in some kinduh pain fo' Godsakes jus' say so!

(Pause.)

RITA: Done shout at me, Tony.

(Pause.)

TONY (quietly): Nobody likes being married to a martyr.

(Pause.)

Where's Binkie?

RITA: He's over at Joyce. It's Michael's birt'day. Frank said he'll bring him back after. I tole you alluh this las' night. Y'memory got more holes than a mosquito net.

TONY: You made sure the chile wrap up warm?

RITA: It's jus' over the road, Tony, it's not the Antarctic. Anyway he's five years old. He'll soon be old enough to *vote*.

TONY: Loopy Loo makin' jokes, eh? You swallowed a joke book, Loopy Loo.

(Pause. Loudly.)

This is Shepherd's Bush, not Port o' Spain, Trinidad. That's not sunshine out there, woman . . . !

(Then.)

Only the English would call a night like this *Spring*. They do it in memory of their *fondest* hour. *Dunkirk*.

(Pause.)

RITA: Look, you want y'dinner or not?

(Pause.)

TONY: Done bother me.

(He stretches. Slumps. Pause. Pushes his work aside. Quiet whining.)

I shouldn't have to. After I come home from that factory I shouldn't have to frig aroun' all night with this.

(Suddenly sweeps a number of transistors and screwdrivers on the floor.)

Christ, man, all I do is work!

RITA (crying out): An' you think I'm not tired too? You complain about me being *sleepy*, but you done think I got *cause*? All day long I'm on m'feet, I'm not any chargehan' you know, sittin' on m'ass all day. I got to be up an' down, up an' down, then when I come home I got to stand in frontuh the hot stove out there, cookin' his lordship's dinner! An' then as you come in you start complainin'. What you take me for, some sortuh machine? Wondawoman? You think I done feel tired like everybody else? You think so?!

(Pause.)

You think so?!

(Pause.)

TONY: OK, OK, so this is no life for a woman. But I buy you things, done I? What more you want? A holiday in Las Vegas?!

RITA: Things! Things!

TONY: You think all this drop from heaven. Radiogram - Tee Vee - tape recorder - you think they drop from heaven?

RITA: Fo' me? A tape recorder! You buy that tape recorder fo' me? What would I do wit' a tape recorder, boy? Tape you when you asleep - snorin'?!

(Pause.)

Anyway, you din' buy it in the firse place, you made it.

TONY: I done want no more rudeness from you - put y'dress back on. Before I lose m'temper, woman.

(Pause.)

RITA: It won't be the firse time you lost y'temper.

(Pause. TONY rises. Crosses lazily over to her, smiling dangerously. Pause.)

TONY: I'm jus' the kinduh guy to make a masochist happy, done forget that.

(Pause.)

RITA (unflinching): Mr Big Man. Big Shot. Mr Big Shot.

(Pause.)

TONY (shame, something): Look, jus' put on y'dress, OK? OK?

(Then.)

Jus' done fight me all the time. OK? Please, OK?

(Pause. RITA retrieves her dress. Discards dressing-gown. She and TONY look at each other. TONY goes to her, strokes her arm.)

After six years I still can't keep m'han's off you.

(Pause.)

RITA: You in a bad way then, ain' you?

(And then she moves out of reach. TONY not amused. RITA puts on her dress.)

TONY (involuntary): Why you so perverse, woman . . . !

(Pause.)

RITA: You done own me.

(Pause.)

TONY (surprisingly humble for him): I marry you, Rita; I'm y'husban', woman.

RITA: That means a lotuh things to me, an' I play fair by you. But it done give you a right to own me.

(Pause.)

TONY: No woman ever baffle me like you.

RITA (mocking): That's why you marry me. Right?

(Pause.)

TONY: They do away with the death penalty in England now, done forget that, woman.

(Pause.)

You read me, whore?

RITA: Whore? Yeah? An' who are all these men who had me? Give me their names 'cos they never even bothered to introduce themselves.

(Pause.)

You must be mixin' me up with oneuh them English girls you see at weekends.

TONY: Weekends? English girls? What's this, Loopy Loo? You mean I been walkin' in m'sleep again?

(Pause.)

RITA: Las' Saturday night you din' come home till Sunday afternoon.

(Pause.)

TONY (truculent): You always tell me to go out more, so I follow y'advice.

RITA: I din' mean fo' the whole weekend!

(Pause. TONY sucks his teeth, returns to work-bench. Picks up stuff he knocked on the floor.)

Anyway las' Saturday was nothing special. You been out the week before that, an' the week before that, an' the week before that, an' the week . . . !

TONY: OK!

(Pause.)

So occasionally I stay out a bit *late-ish*.

RITA: *Late-ish*!

TONY: Anyway, Sunday! Not till Sunday! You lucky I ever come back at all.

(Pause.)

RITA: Things are that bad fo' you, eh, boy?

(Sucks her teeth. Pause.)

When you want me, do I often turn away?

TONY: Many times you only put up with me!

RITA: You always hungry; I only hungry *someuh* the time. That's the root of all our troubles.

(She yawns.)

TONY: The root of our troubles is that you're always tired.

(Pause.)

You're not takin' those iron tablets the doctor gave you. If y'sufferin' from anaemia then take the proper medicine.

RITA: Maybe I got an extra reason fo' being so tired these days. I'm pregnant.

(Pause.)

TONY: Come again?

RITA: Pregnant. Never heard of it? It's a habit wit' women. Never caught on wit' men, though. Done ask me why.

(Pause.)

TONY: Are you crazy!

(Pause.)

You forgot a'ready!

(Pause.)

You nearly died las' time!

RITA (simply): I want another chile, Tony . . . I won't stop tryin' till I have one.

TONY: Or till you qualify for a free ride in a hearse.

(Pause. Then.)

Well, one thing's certain: you can't have it. An' that's that.

RITA: What y'mean 'I can't have it!' You think it's the same as buyin' a new dress? You think I can sen' it back to the manufacturers?

TONY (a cry): Rita, it's no joke!

(Pause.)

Havin' another chile could kill you: the doctor spelled it out fo' you.

RITA (gently): Hush. Done be afraid.

(Pause.)

I'll outlive you. I promise.

(Pause.)

TONY: Maybe you should at lease stop work from now.

RITA: You forget you got y'heart set on studyin' accountancy . . . !

TONY: Sure, but I can go at night. I've done it before.

RITA: Tony, done talk rot. It's not easy workin' in the day an' goin' to class at night.

TONY: I did it las' term.

RITA: That was diff'rent. You had to get y'G.C.E.s. But if you want to atten' full-time college now that means you got to go in the day. You got no choice; from this October you gotta stop work. An' that means I have to keep on workin' as long as I can. Right?

(Pause.)

We could never manage, if I done put by some money from now.

TONY: No man should make his wife work herself sick, so he can stop work.

RITA: Boy, you too ole-fashioned.

(Pause.)

TONY (quietly, almost rueful): I dunno how you do it, girl. Any time I need money fo' anything it's always you who save it up.

RITA (simply): Tony, anything you want you must have. Once it's in my power to help you get it . . . you're m'husban'.

(Pause.)

TONY: I never met a woman like you.

RITA: You lucky.

(Pause.)

TONY: Even the radiogram. I talk a lotuh nonsense about it, but we're only able to afford it causeuh you.

(Pause. Almost sadly.)

I could never save a penny if I din' have you.

RITA: Yes, well. Anyway once you go through wit' it this time, I done mine. Workin' an' savin', I mean. If you sure that's what you want to be, an accountant, well fine.

TONY (crying out): I done want to handle record-players all my life . . . !

RITA: But you got a talent fo' buildin' them. That's why all y'frien's want one. Each time you build another set I feel prouduh you, Tony. Proud, proud.

TONY: That done cut no ice wit' the Midlan' Bank! When anybody ask what's my occupation? I want to be able to say 'accountant an' done you forget it'. Not 'I'm a chargehan' who builds record-players'. When you're an accountant people call you sir, when you handle record-players all they do is call you names. Right? Am I right?

(Pause.)

Makin' tape recorders, record-players, that's a boy's game, accountancy makes you a *man*.

RITA (sad about it): Whatever pleases you, Tony, it's up to you. I'll help as much as I can.

(Pause.)

TONY (a cry): It's not a dream, Loopy Loo . . . !

(Pause.)

As an accountant I could make three, maybe four thousan' a year. Four thousan', Loopy Loo! Wit' that kind of money we could buy a little house, 'invest in a property'. A place where we could have room to invite frien's. Not like this - *storeroom*.

(Pause.)

You couldn't even invite the Thin Man here. Even if he went on a *diet*.

(Pause.)

Girl, we could really start to live, if only we had our own place. No more goin' out in a cold, cold passage jus' to do toilet. We'll have a toilet nex' to the bedroom. A centrally *heated* toilet! Gorgeous! The whole place would be centrally heated. Ow, Loops . . . ! Happiness is a house with central heatin' - from top to bottom!

(Pause.)

Think of it, once we could afford it, we need never freeze in Englan' again. This country would be a different place all-together! Imagine it - imagine bein' so warm you gotta turn *down* the heat. BEAU-TI-FUL!

(Pause.)

Four thousan'. It's not like wantin' a million. There are guys who pay that much in *TAX*!

(Pause.)

Some white women spend more than that on a neck-liss. One neck-liss. Then they leave it lying aroun' so any and everybody could steal it!

(Pause. Bitter laugh.)

You gotta laugh. The whole pattern is so *unfair*, it's almost *funny*. Man.

(Pause.)

Ole God, eh, Sweet Pea. He really got it in fo' black people. No doubt about it. He rather see all of us freezin' in a room in *Shepherd's Bush* - wrap up in a overcoat like a cocoon - than see us wrap up in central heatin', warm as a butterfly.

(Pause.)

No lie, Rita. There just gotta be a God.

(Another private laugh.)

I mean the black man been put down fo' so long - that can't be jus' coincidence.

(His jaundiced laughter trails away. Pause.)

They even talk to you diff'rent when you makin' that kinduh money. White people. You done have to take as much crap from them. If only 'cos they know with that money you can afford a good law-yer! An' in any white court havin' a good law-yer is better than being innocent!

(He laughs, boyishly. Pause.)

Four, five years. That's all it'll take to be a Certified Accountant. Four, maybe five years.

(Dismissing even the thought of failure with a wave of his hand.)

I should do that easy. Easy, easy. It's simply a matteruh retaining the right facts. Anybody could do it. Once they apply themselves.

(Pause.)

Then after I get m'degree I'm in business, Loopy Loo! I'm laughin'!

(Pause.)

I'll only work fo' Jews. An' they got to be rich Jews or I'll practise anti-semitism.

(Laughs a he-he-he laugh. Pause. Then.)

Jews an' nobody else! I got respect fo' Jews. Jews *know.* An' what they know is how to *survive.* Copy the Jews. That's all I gotta say to West Indians.

(Pause.)

Strictly fo' Jews. No Wasps. You got to draw the line somewhere, Loopy.

(He gives another soft, jaundiced laugh. Pause.)

Four thousan'. Nothin' fantastic.

(Pause.)

A little house with nice central heatin' . . . Binkie could have his own room . . . you could buy y'self some good clothes, Rita.

(Pause.)

Four thousan'. Compared to what some people want from life that's sweet F.A. It would do me, though.

(Snickering.)

I'd make do with four thousan' a year any day.

(Pause. RITA goes to dressing table. Brings out a cigar.)

RITA: Here, make do with this, Mr Onassis. I got it fo' you today.

TONY: Loopy Loo, you're a queen!

(He unwraps cigar. She produces a box of matches. Gives him a light for his cigar.)

You spoil me, Rita.

(He puffs away, happy as a Captain of Industry.)

RITA (almost sadly): Jus' persevere. If *you* want a thing bad enough who knows . . . ? You might be unlucky enough to get it.

(TONY blows a smoke ring. Pause.)

TONY: You needn't work so hard though, girl. I done like to see it.

(Pause.)

It's so asinine! OK, so we need to put by the money. But I could get it easy, easy - without you killin' y'self out.

RITA (testy): So what you sugges'?

TONY (beaming): The horses, girl! What else?

(Pause.)

RITA (moving away): I'll get y'dinner. I hope you choke on it.

TONY: Rita!

(She stops. Pause.)

Wht's a fifty pence bet between frien's?

RITA: You never stop at a fifty pence bet!

(Pause.)

TONY: When I start messin' about with the rent an' the food money, *that's* when you gotta worry.

(Pause. She puts her hand on the door-knob.)

Loops, how often have I nearly won big, big money? How often?

RITA: Nearly! A horse that nearly win a race is a horse that lost.

TONY (boisterously): Done be so technical, Loopy Loo!

(Pause.)

Come'ere.

(He crosses to her.)

Sit down, come on.

(Puts his arm across her shoulder, leads her back to armchair, the last great charm boys.)

Comfortable?

(Pause.)

Loopy Loo, have I ever lied to you?

RITA: Yes.

TONY: You being technical again, woman.

(Pause.)

RITA: Boy, I'm not amused.

(Pause. But her defences are weak.)

TONY: Kiss me, Queen Victoria.

(Pause. She kisses him softly.)

RITA: No other man ever touch me, Tony, you do believe that . . . done you?

TONY: Listen, Rita, Little Prince run today. At nine to one!

(RITA sucks her teeth, turns her head away. TONY oblivious.)

Nine to one. What've I always tole you about a nine-to-one horse?

(She faces him again.)

RITA: You mean you had a bet today! Despite all you said!

TONY: Talk sense. You forget I done get paid until tomorrow. Which bookie you know would allow me to place a bet without money? You know any bookie that mad?!

RITA: Good, I'm glad. You mighta throw away y'money.

TONY (as if he is trying to keep calm because he knows he's dealing with someone who's mentally subnormal, and it's not her fault): How do I throw 'way money on a horse that starts at nine to one? How many times have you heard me say that a nine-to-one horse is lucky fo' me? You might laugh but it's a dead cert as far as I'm concerned. A dead, dead cert! It's bound to win. Bound to. Once it *starts* at that price I done care who's the fav'rite - that horse at nine-to-one odds bound to win!

RITA: Superstition.

(Pause.)

TONY (not taking the bait): You think so? Yeah? Superstition?

(Sucks his teeth.)

OK, if you feel facts is superstition, that's your problem. It works fo' me, that's all I know. I'll tell you this, woman, I'd bet all m'clothes on a horse that starts at nine-to-one odds.

RITA: In this country they lock you up if they ketch you runnin' aroun' nakkid. Bear that in mine before you go about makin' all kinduh stupid bet.

TONY (wearily): I'm talkin' to you about something serious to me, an' all you got fo' me is jokes.

(He turns away. Brings out his son's xylophone. Picks out a tune.)

RITA: Waituh minute . . . ! You sure you din' have a bet, boy? You say you had no money but did you *borrow* any?

(Pause.)

TONY (singing: tapping out some kind of tune on xylophone): I'm dreamin' of a BLACK Chris'mus!

(Pause.)

That oughtuh sell a million copies in Harlem - what you think, Loopy Loo?

(Pause. Loudly.)

It's my money, *my* money. I done have to answer to you fo' nothing!

(Pause.)

RITA (mildly): OK, Tony.

(Pause.)

TONY: OK, I borrow a poun' from Frank - one poun'! Report me to the C.I.A.

(Pause. He can't keep a straight face.)

All this fuss. Done you prefer to see me in the arms of a horse than in the arms of an English girl?

(Pause.)

RITA (giving nothing): It's a free country. Do what you want.

(Pause.)

TONY: Bitch. It was jus' a joke.

RITA: Grow up, Tony, f'Godsakes.

TONY (stung): Bitch - you hate to see me happy!

RITA (infuriatingly): Oh yes?

TONY: You only have to see a smile on m'face an' you're sure to throw a bucketuh cold water all over me. Bitch.

RITA: That the only word you know? Bitch!

TONY: Women drain a man. They never satisfy until they got a man wit' his throat cut an' his blood *drainin'* away. They oughtuh employ women in them places where they slaughter cattle. They'd teach the men a thing or two.

RITA (untouched, almost amused by him): Boy, you fulluh shit.

TONY: Yes, I know. Everybody but you.

(Pause.)

All these years an' I still dunno where I stan' wit' you. I'm not stone! I'm not a pieceuh *wood*. I gottuh right to know how m'own wife feel about me.

(Pause.)

If I said to you I was goin' to leave you to shack up wit' a dozen women all you'd do is han' me m'hat an' m'coat.

RITA: What you expect me to do - beg you to stay?

TONY (crying out): An' why not . . . ! You're m'wife!

(Pause.)

RITA: I never betray you yet, you betray me countless times a'ready. Countless!

(Pause.)

TONY: I still tell you I love you, I feed you the words over an' over again.

RITA: Yes - words, words!

TONY (shouting): An' what's wrong wit' words!

RITA: They breed lies like germs!

(Pause.)

TONY (quietly, deadly): I'll make you say it, bitch, one day I'll make you say you love me. I'll break you in yet, bitch!

(Pause.)

RITA: An' you say you love me.

(TONY pounds the xylophone with the sticks, his frustration boiling over.)

TONY: Break you! Break you! Break - you! I - *swear* - it!

(He stops. Worn down. Pause.)

RITA: Boy, if you ain' mad, well I dunno.

(Pause.)

TONY (vulnerable): I'm alone in this country, Rita, if I can't be sureuh you I might as well let them sen' m'back home.

RITA (sad smile): Leave me the radiogram before you go.

(TONY slaps her; the side of her face. Nothing vicious, it is just a warning blow. She does not even raise her hand to her face. Pause. He tries to embrace her. She holds him off.)

Leave me be. I'll get y'dinner.

(RITA goes out to kitchen (off). TONY goes to his overcoat behind the door. He produces an evening paper from one of the pockets. He turns to Racing Pages. Begins to write out a bet.)

TONY: Kempton . . . two forty-five . . . My Girl. Eleven to -

(He hears RITA returning. Hides paper under the bed. RITA opens the door. Stands in doorway holding her stomach.)

RITA: Tony.

(She is evidently in some pain.)

TONY: Girl, what's wrong?

(He hurries to her. Helps her sit down.)

RITA: Something's gone wrong. Get Dr Thomas. QUICK.

(Quick blackout.)

Scene Two

House in Shepherd's Bush. The FLETCHERS' room. Summer. Day.

Room looks rather neglected. Bed unmade etc. TONY has not progressed very far with the record-player. He has attached a turn-table to the motor now but that's all. TONY lets himself in. He is in a great hurry. He is carrying a large Coke. Deposits it. He rushes around the room tidying up. He removes all obvious traces of RITA as well. He stuffs their wedding photographs into wardrobe. DENNIS knocks at his door. TONY lets him in. DENNIS is a West Indian student of Sociology. He wears glasses. If he's not careful he will have a nervous breakdown.

DENNIS: Man, Tony, what're you doin'? If you've changed y'mind, it's OK, I'll understand.

TONY: Jus' keep quiet an' help me clean up.

(DENNIS picks up some of TONY's clothes which are on the floor. Holds them up.)

DENNIS: Really missin' Rita, aren't you?

(Pause.)

TONY: So?

DENNIS: Well, it's up to you, y'know, I done mind. I mean about the girls.

TONY: Jus' because I invite another woman up here that done mean I love m'wife less. Anyway it's not my fault Rita had to go into hospital. I mean she might be in there fo' ages, Dennis, what happens to me in the meantime . . . !

(Pause.)

I mean I'm too old fo' cold showers, Dennis.

(Pause.)

DENNIS: I'll go an' get the chicks. They must be dying in the car. Sandra fancies you, I'm sure of it.

TONY: She's got good taste.

(DENNIS laughs, goes. TONY crosses over to the bed, stands over it for a moment, thinking of RITA. He sucks his teeth, sighs, something. Makes up the bed. DENNIS returns with the two girls. One English, one West Indian. The English girl enters first.

SANDRA: blonde, buxom, attractive in a rather obvious way. About twenty-two. Traces of a Yorkshire accent; hip vernacular. Too much make-up is inclined to make her look a bit tarted-up. She is fleshy, and her mini-dress is sleeveless, low-cut. She is well aware that English men prefer their women to be more slender, so she knows who her admirers are. Nothing hard or brassy about her, she is even-tempered, optimistic. She is a not very successful go-go dancer. Has a rather empty, self-conscious laugh.

YVONNE: light-skinned, pretty West Indian girl of about twenty-one. She has no time for any kind of black past. She will marry an English-man some day. Colourful blouse, decorative belt, peach-coloured trousers.)

SANDRA: What's up, man?

TONY: Come in, come in.

SANDRA: We're already in or haven't you noticed?

(Gives her laugh.)

TONY: Comic. Sit anywhere you want.

(The girls sit on the settee. DENNIS remains standing. As does TONY. He hangs his jacket behind the door.)

YVONNE: A bit *cramped*, this room.

TONY: Why, you thinkin'uh buyin' it?

YVONNE: No thanks. I already got a cupboard.

(Pause.)

SANDRA (abruptly, jolly, to TONY): 'So what happened to you? One minute you were with us, the next minute you'd *split*. Haven't got a wife, have you? Where'd you hide her, under the bed?

TONY (an arrogant stare, faint smile): You like the sounduh yuh own voice, right?

SANDRA: I've had it a long time, maybe that's why.

(Pause. They are looking at each other.)

TONY: Siddown, Dennis. I'm not playing 'God Save the Queen'.

DENNIS: Man, let's have some soul.

(TONY sits on the bed.)

TONY: Put on the tape recorder, nuh. What, you're a cripple?

(DENNIS crosses to tape recorder. Puts it on. The music: 'By The Time I Get To Phoenix' by Isaac Hayes (without the long spoken introduction) from his LP 'Hot Buttered Soul'. Other numbers include: 'If There Is A Hell Down Below We're All Gonna Go' by Curtis Mayfield, or any other comparable number by Mayfield. Numbers by Otis Reading, The Temptations, and Smokey Robinson and the Miracles.)

SANDRA (about Isaac Hayes number): Yeah, great, turn it up. Really moves me, that number.

(DENNIS sits in armchair.)

TONY (looking at SANDRA): We got a real soul-sister here, Dennis.

SANDRA (her laugh): Get thee behind me, you.

(Pause.)

DENNIS (not to anyone in particular): Man, it's hot, eh.

SANDRA: Personally I like it when it's hot. I can sit out in the sun and get all nice 'n' brown. I can't stand to look like sliced white bread.

TONY: I know jus' what you mean.

SANDRA (pleased): Shut up, you!

(TONY laughs, rubbing his hands up and down his thighs with almost boyish glee. DENNIS sits hunched in his chair, moving his body back and forth in time to the music.)

TONY: You like rum, Sandra?

SANDRA: In a glass, yeah.

TONY: You chicks better had like rum, that's all I got!

(He laughs alone. Pause.)

YVONNE (to SANDRA): The last of the big spenders.

(The two girls laugh with each other.)

SANDRA: Golden Boy entertains.

(TONY sucks his teeth. Rises.)

TONY (almost to himself, but loud enough): Women, boy. Jesus.

(He has got up to go to the sideboard. But first stops off at tape recorder. He turns volume down. Continues on to sideboard.)

All your fault, Dennis.

DENNIS (you'd think he was being accused of the Great Train Robbery):

What you mean, man? No, man.

TONY (from sideboard he gets out rum, glasses): I could be in the bettin' shop right now.

(With the Coke he has bought he starts mixing rum'n'coke for four.)

YVONNE: Done let us keep you.

SANDRA: A real charmer isn't he?

TONY (still to DENNIS): Do me a favour. Nex' time you see me near a bettin' shop, *ignore* me. Even if you got Miss Englan' waitin' outside in y'car. OK? Cut me dead.

YVONNE (on her feet): Look, I know when I'm not wanted.

TONY: Since when're you Miss Englan'?

(Pause. No love lost between them.)

DENNIS: Relax, Yvonne. The guy's underuh bit of a strain at the moment, dig? That's all.

TONY: Sit down, done mine me, I talk too much. Here.

(Gives YVONNE a drink. She sits down.)

YVONNE (grudgingly): Thanks.

(TONY hands SANDRA and DENNIS their drinks. Sits on the bed.)

DENNIS: Rita's goin' to be all right, man. Trust Uncle Dennis, right? These things are sent to try us, man. I firmly believe that. Not by God - anyuh that rubbish - I done believe in God anymore. I mean once I was a good Catholic boy an' alluh that, but that was before I experience life in this country. You try to believe in God in this country, you jus' try.

(Pause.)

By nature. Not God, nature. To test us, man. To make sure we find it harder to survive. We, as a people.

(Pause.)

SANDRA: What's he on about?

YVONNE: You askin' me . . . ! I done even work here.

TONY (sucking his teeth, almost to himself): An' I coulduh been in the bettin' shop. Mindin' m'own business.

(Sucks his teeth again.)

God give me strength.

SANDRA: What're you mumbling about, man?

TONY: I said so you're a go-go dancer, eh? I wouldn't mind *go-go-going* to bed with you.

SANDRA: Is he always like this?

(Then.)

I dance at Beanos. It's not much of a club but it's home.

TONY: Beanos! Christ! The las' time I went to that club the bouncer asked me for a dance.

SANDRA: Liar! You liar!

TONY: Maybe he wasn't queer, but everytime he had to chuck anybody out he went home wit' them in a taxi.

SANDRA: Oh, you liar!

(They laugh together. Then continue to look at each other. Pause.)

YVONNE: Who's Rita?

(Pause.)

DENNIS: His sister!

TONY: M'sister, yeah, yeah.

(Pause.)

SANDRA: What's wrong with her?

TONY: She's in hospital.

(Pause.)

In all she's been gone about three months now.

SANDRA: God, how terrible for her.

TONY: Yeah, well.

(Pause.)

I see her every evening, y'know.

(Pause. He moves over to BINKIE's photograph.)

That's the boy. Her son. I was lookin' after him, y'know, while she's been away. I couldn't manage, though.

(Pause.)

I had to send him to his gran'mother in Trinidad.

(Pause.)

Like a package.

(Pause.)

You feel you prepared fo' everything. Then something like this happen.

(Sucks his teeth.)

Shoot.

(Pause. More to himself than any of them.)

Man, I can hardly remember a time when there wasn't something goin' wrong ... or when I wasn't out there hustlin' fo' bread by fair means or foul.

(Pause.)

Hustle, hustle, hustle, that's all it's ever been.

(Pause.)

Tryin' to win bread, tryin' not to lose bread. One endless hustle.

(Pause.)

I never had time to learn to trust others, or to think of those worse off than me. I never had time to be anything but hard.

(Pause.)

You gotta be rich to afford them kinduh luxuries.

(Sucks his teeth again. Quietly.)

This room . . . this room.

(Pause. He sits down on bed again. SANDRA offers him her cigarettes.)

SANDRA: Here, help y'self. They're menthol. You shouldn't let things get you down.

TONY (quick cover-up): Get me down . . . ! Me! Not this boy. I done let things get me down. I might be a ass, but I'm not a *mad*ass.

(Pause.)

Once you let life get you by the neck, you might as well take up Hari-Kari. As a hobby.

(Pause.)

DENNIS (abruptly, creating enthusiasm): So how're things, man, Tony? How's the studies goin' eh? You should be startin' full-time college soon, right? September's jus' about a month away.

TONY: Maybe nex' year September. But not this year, that's fo' sure. Everything's changed, how many times I got to tell you that?

DENNIS: But man, you still could've done your studies, even with Rita in hospital.

TONY (guilty outburst): I had to take careuh the chile, you forget.

DENNIS: Yeah, sorry.

(Pause.)

TONY: I jus' got to accept the fact this wasn't my year, that's all. Anyway when you consider the numberuh people takin' accountancy these days maybe it's best I put it off fo' a year or two.

(Pause. The others embarrassed.)

Maybe nex' year. Who knows?

(Pause.)

DENNIS: So what'uve you been doin' with y'self all this time?

TONY: Lotsuh things, man. Lots. Lots.

(Pause.)

There's a lotuh things a man wit' all my money can do in London. Join the Playboy Club, f'example. Or the Conservative Party.

(SANDRA finds the thought of that funny indeed. TONY: wryly.)

You like the thoughtuh that, do you? Eh?

(Pause.)

Yeah.

(Pause. Wearily.)

Or he can always gamble. No man is that poor that a spotuh gamblin' couldn't make him poorer.

DENNIS: I thought as much! You've gone back to heavy gamblin'.

TONY (made angry): What you mean 'heavy gamblin''? Even if every Friday I was to put m'whole week's salary on one horse, not even a pauper would call that heavy gamblin'.

DENNIS: Heavy gamblin' means bettin' more than you can afford.

TONY: That ain't 'heavy gamblin''! That's bein' a coon.

(Only he and SANDRA find that funny. Pause.)

DENNIS: What about all that money you had put by to help pay the fees at that college an' everything? You haven't thrown it all away on the horses, I hope?

TONY (harsh): What gives you that idea?

DENNIS: Be cool, man. No reason to get all hot an' bothered about anything I say.

TONY: Bothered! Me! Get away. Nothing bothers Tony.

(Pause. Abrupt infuriating laugh.)

Yesterday I lost ten quid on a horse. Not even that can bother me!

DENNIS: Ten pounds? An' you reckon that's not heavy gamblin'?

(Pause.)

TONY (bitter-sweet amusement): I was so sure about that horse, sure, sure. When I tell you sure I mean dead sure. Dead, dead sure! An' what happen? The flickin' horse end up in a photo-finish. Six to one, it was. Six to one! I could've won sixty poun's, plus m'ten poun's back. Seventy quid less tax.

(Pause.)

I coulda done wit' that money.

(Pause.)

Seventy quid. An' that horse had to get caught up in a photo-finish.

(Pause.)

Ole God done like Tony. In fact He must hate me.

(Pause.)

I still can't believe it. I got beat by a photograph. A photograph.

(Abrupt, self-mocking laugh.)

It's enough to put me off cameras fo' life!

(Pause.)

I coulduh cried, boy.

DENNIS: Cried! Fo' ten pounds I'd 'ave cut m'throat.

(TONY sticks out his throat.)

TONY: Looky here!

(The others all laugh. But there is some disapproval in DENNIS's laugh.)

DENNIS: You always were a very happy guy, Tony. Happy, happy. Too happy.

(Pause. TONY gets up.)

TONY (getting some kind of jaundiced amusement out of it): I jus' seem to have gone crazy. I mean you won't *believe* it.

(Pause.)

There's jus' been no stoppin' me these las' three months. The bookies should get together an' send me a turkey fo' Christmas.

(Pause. The others aren't laughing.)

One turkey! I reckon they owe me a whole farmyard.

(Pause.)

Not that I always lose, mind you.

(Snickers.)

I jus' done win often enough, that's all . . . !

(And laughs all by himself. Pause.)

DENNIS: Ten poun's. Christ, man. Where do you get the bread? An' you're the guy who's always tellin' me about being in control.

TONY: Ach, I'm still in control.

(Sits.)

Complete control. Some guys put their house an' their car in hock to back horses. But not me. Mainly because I got no house nor car!

(YVONNE waits until he's quiet again.)

YVONNE: You make me sick.

TONY (snickering again): That makes two of us.

YVONNE (loudly): You think it's funny! It's a *sickness*.

(Pause.)

You're playin' into white people's hands!

TONY (quietly): This might come as a surprise to you, girl. I done think it's very funny. But I done think it's a crime neither.

(Pause. To DENNIS.)

Guess who I saw las' week - Oscar.

(He gets up again. Gathers up their glasses.)

DENNIS: That ass!

(TONY crosses to sideboard. Starts mixing them fresh drinks.)

TONY: I was in the bettin' shop roun' the corner, tryin' to decide whether I should make a Yankee bet or not. When in walks Oscar, large as life an' twice as loud. Right away he asks me to lend him a poun'. Months I ain' see the guy. Months. An' the first words he hits me with is - 'len' me a poun', Tony'! After that I knew I might as well jus' forget that Yankee.

DENNIS: That guy's a *blight*.

TONY: A blight! He's a one-man epidemic. He ought to be put in a isolation ward - fo' life!

(Pause.)

Len' him a poun' . . . !

(Sucking his teeth.)

He gets me so *vex*, that boy. Vex, vex.

(Pause.)

I mean when I win I'm prepared to len' a guy *five* poun's. Right? But before a race done bother me. If it's one thing I've had to learn from *bitter* experience it's that once you len' somebody money *durin'* gamblin' you sure to lose. He takes your luck away.

YVONNE: They ought to take you away. To a padded cell.

TONY: I suppose you call that superstition, right?

YVONNE: Wrong, I call it madness.

TONY (a sigh, he's dealing with another of the uninitiated): You wouldn't understan', you're a non-believer. You got to believe in gamblin' to understan' gamblin'. You gotta believe in all the rules. All gamblers got their own beliefs, their own signs: some gamblers done like to hear or watch the race they bettin' on, others think it's bad luck to drop anything when they're in the bettin' shop, even if it's jus' a pieceuh paper. You can dismiss such things as superstition but to a gambler it's the difference between good luck an' bad luck.

(Pause.)

YVONNE: I never heard such drivel in m'whole life.

TONY (above it all): Per'aps. Per'aps.

(Pause.)

SANDRA: Racing, that's not my scene, man.

TONY: What's your scene, Minnie Mouse?

(Pause.)

SANDRA: That depends on what you're selling?

(Pause. They are looking at each other.)

YVONNE (looking away, under her breath): West Indian men.

TONY: Pardon?

(Pause. Some hostility between him and YVONNE.)

YVONNE (turning in DENNIS's direction): I could do with a turn-on. You still have that joint on you?

TONY (flatly): I done want you smokin' here, please.

YVONNE (a great sigh as she faces him): What's this now?

TONY: I done hold with drugs. Sorry an' all that. What you do outside is your business, but I live here. OK?

(Pause.)

YVONNE (quiet dislike): You ever try getting a job with the Vice Squad?

TONY: You want m'work number? It's 999.

YVONNE: I'll call you the next time I need a headache.

TONY: Fo' you I'd even arrange a head transplant.

(Pause. YVONNE gets up.)

YVONNE: Dennis, I'm going!

(TONY's laugh is infuriatingly mocking.)

DENNIS (he does not move from bed): Oh, f'Chrisesake, woman.

YVONNE: You coming or not?

(Pause. DENNIS rises, sucking his teeth.)

DENNIS: I see you, brother. Stay cool, OK?

TONY: Man, look, sit down.

(YVONNE has gone to the door. SANDRA has not moved.)

YVONNE: You coming, Dennis Tait?

DENNIS: Yeah, yeah.

(YVONNE opens the door.)

YVONNE (to TONY): At least I don't spend my life in a British bettin' shop. I have some pride.

TONY (touching an imaginary forelock): God bless you.

(YVONNE storms out. Disappears down the passage.)

DENNIS: How about you, Sandra?

SANDRA: I'll stay. I'll be OK. Go and comfort her.

(Pause.)

DENNIS: Right, please y'self.

(TONY rises. Goes to window.)

You OK, man?

(Pause.)

TONY (at window): There's this chick, y'know . . . every morning when I'm goin' to work I see her at the tube station. She's always by herself. A nice, nice chick. Coloured. A well-dressed black chick, I mean *really* well-dressed. Gorgeous, boy. Like a model, y'know. Only . . . only she always *screams* and *screeches* at everybody. Screeches at them in some strange, mad tongue.

(Pause. Sucks his teeth.)

Jesus, boy.

(Pause.)

You should see how those English people pretend they can't see her . . . her distress.

(Pause.)

Lord only knows how long she's been in this country.

(Pause. Tapping his forehead.)

In here. She's gone *in here.*

(Pause. Hard, disgruntled.)

People talk about how we can't get proper jobs in this country, decent accommodation. But what nobody as yet really knows about is the price we're payin' *up here.* We're not even *aware* of someuh the pressures. But it's all takin' it's toll; right *here.*

(Pause.)

The way I see it, what's important, as far as we're concerned, is *not* that the English see us as the challenger. But that we see them as the champ. An' you can deny that all y'want, but it's that fact that our *mines* have gotta absorb *daily.* Like a kick in the crotch. It's no wonder that *up here* we sometimes short circuit under the strain. It's no joke to know you gotta be able to knock out the other guy, before the ref will even call the fight a draw.

(Pause. Almost to himself.)

Look about London. Look at the numberuh black people babblin' away to themselves, it's a cryin' shame.

(Pause. Then.)

An' since a lotuh English people aren't too sane neither, then God help us.

(And gives a laugh of sorts.)

Jus' think what that means eh? Our safe-conduc' depen's on one helluv an assumption, *that they'll never go completely mad.*

(Quietly.)

There's so few of us an' so manyuh them.

(Pause.)

OK, sure they'd say such a thing could never happen. What with their well-known stiff upper lip an' everything. *But how do I know that*?

(Quiet cry.)

It's my life that's being laid on the line here!

(Pause. He can't keep a straight face.)

An' if my safety depen's on nothing more than *somebody else's* upper lip, then that's hardly guarantee to do my sanity much good. Right? Right!

(He and DENNIS laugh together; whether they are very amused or not is another matter.)

I mean, buddy, you ever see someuh them football crowds when they *descend* on London fo' a match. Eh?! You'd have to look pretty far to find even one stiff upper lip among that lot.

(Their laughter renews itself. Dies away. Pause. Then hard, cold again.)

So you tell her this fo' me, that girl down there, tell her it helps me manage. That's why I do it. Gamble. It helps me survive. Gamblin' helps keep me on an . . . *even keel* . . .

(Taps his forehead again.)

. . . . up here.

(Pause.)

Once you got a passion, the odds are in your favour.

(Pause.)

They're not goin' to make a eunuch outa me. Not this boy. Not if I can help it.

(Pause.)

DENNIS (at door): Take it easy, man, Tony. OK?

(Then.)

See you, Sandra.

(DENNIS waves, goes. Pause.)

SANDRA: Cigarette?

(TONY has not moved from his vigil by the window.)

TONY: What? Oh, no, no thanks.

(TONY moves from window over to sideboard. Pours a little rum in his glass.)

Want some moreuh this?

(And not waiting for a reply crosses to her and adds some rum to her glass.)

SANDRA: Thanks.

(TONY sits in armchair.)

You're an interesting sort of bloke, aren't you?

TONY (quite mocking): Reckon so, do you?

(SANDRA looks at the drink in her hand. She watches it swirling around in her glass as she speaks.)

SANDRA: Pretty potent stuff, isn't it?

(Pause.)

All this black anger.

(Only then does she look at him. Pause. Then a nod in the direction of his workbench.)

What are you building?

TONY: Who? Oh, that. A record-player.

(More to himself than to her.)

Haven't even finished it yet.

(Pause.)

I can usually build oneuh those things in about a month. Jus' workin' at nights, after work, y'know. But I jus' haven't had the time recently.

(A sigh.)

What with havin' to go to that hospital an' everything.

(Pause.)

It jus' done pay to plan ahead.

(Pause.)

I gotta get holduh some bread. No two ways about it. A quick killin' that's the tonic I need. The right money on the right horse.

(Pause.)

SANDRA: Horses, horses, horses. I can hardly credit it.

(Pause.)

When do I start to fight for my white virtue, that's what I want to know?

(Pause, impish.)

You call y'self a black man?

(Pause.)

TONY: Sixty poun's I could've had now. That horse coulda won easy, easy. That jockey play the ass, that's why.

SANDRA: No racialist worth his salt would believe this.

TONY (rubbing his hands together, suddenly acknowledging her presence): Well, how're you, eh, Minnie Mouse!

(He gets up.)

SANDRA: I'm OK. How're you?

TONY: You got nice thighs.

(Sinks down beside her. He's on the prowl now.)

SANDRA: I thought you'd never notice.

(He plays with her hand, then works his way up her arm, massaging, caressing.)

Do you mind!

(But doesn't remove his hand.)

TONY: Gorgeous.

(The buzzer in his room sounds.)

Aww, Chrise, Dennis musta come back. You want to go?

(Pause. He still has his hand on her arm.)

SANDRA: Do you want me to go?

(Pause.)

TONY: Course not.

(Pause.)

SANDRA: Then I didn't hear any bell. Did you?

TONY: Bell? What bell?

(Pause.)

SANDRA: So how come you've been actin' like some English gent ever since we've been alone?

(Pause. TONY's hand freezes on her arm.)

TONY: Me? An English gent? You gotta be jokin'.

(Pause. He removes his hand.)

I got m'reasons. Maybe I done wanna do anything in this room.

SANDRA: You don't think my thighs are too fat?

TONY: Woman, done talk rubbish. I like to see a woman wit' nice, heavy thighs. Or else where's the diff'rence between women and men?

SANDRA: English men like their women skinny.

TONY (a little laugh): Good, I glad. That leaves all the more women fo' me.

(He hears someone putting a key in the lock.)

Who's that!

(RITA enters. TONY jumps up.)

Girl, what you doin' here!

(Pause. Somehow RITA looks less pregnant than one would expect her to be.)

RITA: I discharge m'self. I wanted to come home. Where there wasn't no white people about!

(Pause.)

Scene Three

The FLETCHERS' room. Summer. Evening.

The room is tidy again. RITA alone in the room polishing glass-top table. She has to stop; she still does not seem very well. She crosses to wardrobe, brings out BINKIE's xylophone. Pause. She places it on the bed. Plays it softly. Stops. Pause. She traces her hand over it sadly. Kneels, burying her face in the bed. Pause.

She hears TONY returning and quickly gets to her feet. TONY enters. They look at each other. Pause. TONY is as usual tie-less.

RITA (quietly): Soon be his birt'day.

TONY: Who?

RITA: His birt'day. Binkie. We'll get 'im something nice . . . OK? An' a card wit' a lion on it.

(Pause. TONY hangs up his jacket.)

TONY: Put that thing away it'll only make you feel worse.

RITA: Remember when you bought it fo' 'im? Remember how I nagged you when you tole me how much you paid fo' it?

(He has crossed to bed to change his shoes.)

TONY: Where's m'shoes?

(Pause. RITA sighs, puts xylophone away. TONY concerns himself with his shoes. Finally.)

You been feelin' OK, Loopy Loo?

RITA: Yeah. Sure.

(She sits in armchair. Sucks her teeth softly. Pause.)

TONY: Had y'medicine?

RITA (rising; preoccupied): Boy, stop botherin' me, y'hear me. I'll get y'dinner.

(She opens the door. Pause. Faces him.)

You'll never know how I feel not havin' that boy here. I miss Binkie so much. Especially now.

(Pause.)

I dunno what I'll do if I lose this baby.

(Pause.)

TONY (loud guilt): Wasn't my fault we had to sen' Binkie to y'mother, jus' done forget that!

RITA: I wasn't away a lifetime . . . !

TONY: You blame me?!

(Pause.)

RITA: I want m'boy chile near me, that's all I'm sayin'.

TONY (crying out): You have me, Rita . . . ! I'm here.

(Pause. She goes off to kitchen. Pause. TONY turns on the tape recorder. RITA returns with his dinner, deposits it on glass-top table. She has brought in a beer with his meal; she pours it out for him. He turns tape recorder off. He comes over to sit down. RITA moves away. Pause. He picks at his food.)

I suppose now fo' the restuh the night we'll jus' sit an' watch Tee Vee.

(Pause. Then a snicker.)

It's no wonder so many young white people envy black people, it's the full, vital life we lead.

(RITA ignores him. Pause.)

I done feel like eatin'.

(Pause.)

They hire a new guy at work today. I dunno where they find the guy. He dunno a thing about amplifiers. To tell you the honest truth the guy dunno a thing about nothing! Naturally he's a student.

(Pause.)

I hate Tuesdays. Everybody else hate Mondays, but I got to be diff'rent.

(Pause.)

Friday is payday; Monday is the day you wonder what happen to the weekend. But what's a *Tuesday*?

(Pause. Snickering.)

Tuesday is not a day it's a *punishment*.

(Pause.)

Come to thinkuh it, I done much care fo' Thursdays, neither.

(And guffaws boyishly. Then.)

You like that, Loops? You like m'lecture on the daysuh the week? Eh?

(She ignores him. His genial mood dies out.)

I'm talkin' to you, woman.

(Pause.)

Rita!

(Pause.)

Only white women punish their men by not talkin' to them!

(Pause. Worn down.)

Bitch.

(Pause. Almost a plea.)

Talk to me, Rita. Done turn away.

(Pause. Sad, wistful.)

No cigars fo' me today? Done you have no cigars hidden away like a squirrel?

(Pause. Almost to himself.)

I never was easy to live with.

(Pause. Loudly.)

I din' touch that English girl, how many times I gotta tell you that!

(Pause.)

I shoulda really given you something to complain about.

(Shouting.)

I shoulda had her stripped *naked*, her legs wide open, her blonde pie exposed like it was *SUPPERTIME!* Then you woulda had something to complain about!

(Pause. He gets up, glass in hand. A bit patronising in his wooing.)

Come on, be nice. Look I even left you some beer, Loops.

(She moves away, he follows her, crazy as a fox.)

Comeon, you know you can't hate y'daddy. Eh, Loopy Loo? Not a finger. I wouldn't lay a finger on a white girl. M'whole han', yes. But one finger, never.

(He has managed to jump in front of her. Pause.)

RITA (quietly): Tony, done depress me. Enough is enough.

(Pause.)

It's that money, that's what makes me sick, not some white girl.

(Pause.)

TONY: Money? What money?

(But moves out of her reach just in case. Pause.)

RITA: You take me fo' a real fool, right?

(Pause.)

The money I save up like some ass, that's what money. Din' you think I'd fine out?

(Pause.)

You throw it away on the horses, right?

TONY: Horses! How y'think Binkie got to Trinidad? On an envelope! You think he *store away* on a postage stamp! I had to pay more than halfuh that money on his passage - you forget!

(RITA sits down on settee.)

RITA (mildly): Sure, I know that, but where's the restuh it?

TONY: Rest! What rest! Restuh what? Rest!

(Pause.)

RITA: Ninety-five poun's.

TONY: You've got at least fifteen poun's left - what ninety-five poun's you talkin' about?

RITA: OK, eighty poun's.

(Pause.)

What have you done with it? You seem to have gone insane since I been away.

(Pause.)

TONY: I must be hearin' things. I thought I was in my own room, my own home, but apparently this is some *police station*. New Scotland Yard!

(Pause.)

You want me to empty m'pockets? Done you have any pot you want to plant on me?!

(Pause.)

RITA: Eighty poun's.

(Shaking her head over him.)

Honest to God, Tony.

(Pause.)

TONY (a cry): You baffle me . . . ! You done even lose y'temper.

(Pause.)

You done even care enough about me to shout at me! You done give a damn about me!

(Pause.)

RITA: Maybe I've had to put up wit' so much from you, I jus' can't be
bothered anymore. You're not worth me losin' m'temper.

(Pause.)

TONY (guiltily): I never spent it on horses, fool! I had to pay off back rent!
I owed rent! Rent, stupid, not gamblin' . . . ! Rent, rent.

(Pause.)

RITA: You should see y'self. You look like an advertisement fo' some
all-night horror film.

(Pause.)

Anyway how come you owe all this rent? Eh? Cosuh y'gamblin', right?

(Pause.)

So what's the diff'rence? Either way it's the bookie who's laughin'.

(Pause.)

TONY (a bit overbearing, not loudly): Ach, done bug me. One day you
win, one day you lose. You never know y'luck.

RITA (sudden dislike): I'm sick to my *stomach* hearin' about your luck.

(Pause.)

TONY (vulnerable little laugh): You should neveruh married me then, right?

(Pause.)

RITA (not particularly loud): Sometimes I wish to Jesus I hadn't.

(Pause. TONY backs away from her like an old man, he feels behind
him for something solid to hold onto, a chair, a bed, a wheelchair. He
lowers himself on the bed. Pause.)

Boy, is that suppose to impress me? That little act you jus' perform
there?

(Pause.)

Can't take it, can you? You can dish it out, but y'can't take it. Right?

TONY (he still can't focus): I'm not easy to live with . . . I know. But I
never set out to cripple others . . . that's not my game.

(Pause.)

RITA (quietly): Boy, you're too weak, tha's your trouble.

(Pause.)

TONY (not loudly at first): This room . . . this room.

(Getting to his feet.)

I never been anything but lonely in this country.

(Prowling the room.)

Lonely, lonely! OK, so the money's better an' the education . . . !But the - *price*!

(He stumbles blindly into armchair. Gives it a shove out of his way.)

This room is too small for me!

RITA: Tony!

TONY (unhearing): Sometimes I want to howl! I done have to be the big *hustler* everybody thinks I am. Howl! Jus' let it all out. But who'll hear me? Who wants to know? You go in oneuh their churches an' you lucky if they done have you on a cross before the collection plate even come aroun'!

(Pause.)

One visit to an English church an' you're an atheist fo' life. Life!

(Pause. To RITA. Quieter.)

As fo' you. How much comfort do I get from you? Eh?

(Quiet cry.)

I done even know where I stan' with you anymore. You got me on a string like a yo-yo! Christ, man, Christ!

RITA (rising, her hands out to him): Be quiet. Come here.

TONY (brushing her off like a fly): *Han's off.*

(Quietly deadly.)

I'll get you y'money. Every cent. I'll get you y'flickin' money!

(He grabs for his tie, swings it around his neck, starts tying it furiously.)

To listen to you anyone would think I was oneuh them West Indian *jig-aboos* who divide their time between the pub an' the bettin' shop. I never been on the dole fo' *one day* in this country. Never, never.

RITA (fearful): Tony, what you doin'?

TONY: I'm goin' to get y'money, bitch.

RITA: It wasn't all *my* money.

TONY: Now you remember? Oh yes?

(He is putting on his jacket. She holds on to his arm.)

RITA: Please!

TONY (quiet warning): Leggo, woman.

(Pause. She lets go of him. Pause. He opens the door.)

RITA: Tony.

(He hears it in her voice. Turns.)

TONY: Oh, Lord, what now?

RITA: Something's gone wrong again, do something, Tony.

(TONY has to help her sit down on the bed. He returns to the door and closes it slowly. His eyes survey their room: he is not going anywhere.)

ACT TWO

Scene One

House in Shepherd's Bush. Passage outside the FLETCHERS' room. Summer Day.

We see the back of OSCAR first. He is wearing tight red trousers and red shirt. He knocks at TONY's door. Pause. He peers through the keyhole. Knocks again. Again he peers through the keyhole. Unseen by OSCAR, TONY comes up the stairs behind him.

TONY: Oscar, I'm not at home.

(OSCAR straightens up, startled.)

OSCAR: I dropped a shillin'.

TONY: An' it rolled through the keyhole, right?

OSCAR: You saw it happen, eh? Good, you owe me five pence.

(TONY doesn't even bother to reply; he unlocks his door.)

TONY: I'm glad you could make it, Oscar, I need a favour.

(OSCAR turns and heads for home.)

OSCAR: I got no money.

(TONY brings him back.)

TONY: The day I ask you fo' money, Oscar, is the day I take up suicide.

(TONY leads OSCAR into the room and into a chair.)

OSCAR: Got any straights?

(TONY sucks his teeth, offers his pack of cigarettes.)

How come you home on a Wednesday?

(OSCAR is helping himself to at least three cigarettes. TONY rescues them firmly.)

TONY: You only got one mouth, Oscar.

OSCAR: Jus' testin' you.

(Pause.)

TONY: How come *you're* not at work?

OSCAR: I workin' nights now. Nex' question.

TONY (loudly): Jus' shut up, Oscar, Christ, man, Christ.

(Pause.)

Rita's sick again. She's downstairs with Mrs Frazier. She couldn't sleep las' night, an' the doctor came this mornin'. He made me phone fo' an ambulance. She has to go back to hospital. But up to now no ambulance. Nearly two hours an' still no ambulance. It's got me so worried.

(Pause.)

Anyway, I can't leave her, that's why I need y'help.

OSCAR: Sure, sure, man, anything.

TONY: I want you to put on a bet fo' me.

(Pause. OSCAR gets up.)

OSCAR (quietly): Boy, you're not an ordinary bastard.

(Pause. He moves over to TONY's tape recorder. Turns it on.)

TONY: Will you turn that flickin' thing off!

(OSCAR switches it off. Returns to his seat.)

OSCAR: I mean, she's y'*wife*, man.

TONY: I know she's m'wife. I was at the weddin', remember!

(Pause.)

We need the money. OK! We need the money.

(Pause.)

She had some money put by, but . . . I had a few bad horses, an', well, mostuh the money jus' went.

(Sad.)

You know how it is.

(Sits, pause. He looks surprisingly . . . alone.)

You can't win 'em all, as they say.

(Pause.)

You can't help tryin', tho'. Once you pick one or two winners there's no holdin' y'back. Only . . . you can't expect others to understan' that.

(Pause.)

I never was a easy person to live with.

(Pause.)

That woman is oneuh the few good things that ever happen to me. An' yet the way I treat that girl sometimes . . .

(Sucks his teeth.)

. . . shit.

(Pause.)

I never was easy to live with.

(Pause.)

It's not jus' the money, neither. Not always. It's the winnin' itself. The *uplift* . . . y'know what I mean?

(Brightening.)

Seein' or listenin' to them horses *poundin'* away, knowin' that you back the winner, watchin' them chalk up the results afterwards on the board in the bettin' shop - beau-ti-ful! Too beau-ti-ful. At such times, boy, I feel on *top*. Top, top! Everybody needs something to keep their spirits up. I done care if they happen to be royalty! They need that something to keep their spirits up.

(Pause.)

OSCAR: OK, man, OK, I'll do it.

TONY (blessing him): The Lord bless y', Oscar.

OSCAR: Boy, you're a real hustler . . . ! A real sweet-talkin' man.

TONY: Who, me? Nah. Not me.

(But laughs all the same. Then.)

Anyway, anyway, Oscar, here's what I want you to do. I got fifteen poun's, right?

OSCAR: Fifteen poun's!

TONY: Tha's the lastuh the money.

OSCAR: You mean you ain' satisfy to lose *mostuh* the girl's money, you want to lose *all!*

TONY: Oscar, that's my business, Oscar. OK?

(Pause.)

You see that red shirt you got on, Oscar, an' them red trousers? If I report you to the American Embassy, they'd arrest you as a communist. Immediately, if not sooner!

(Pause.)

As fo' y'trousers being so godalmighty *tight* - they sure to throw the book at y'! Add that to the fact that you *black* as well - well Jesus, boy, they'd have you in the Electric Chair by nightfall!

OSCAR: Boy, you too fanciful.

TONY (a moment's exhaustion, something): Yeah . . . ? Fanciful? Then all I gotta say is that you haven't looked at the Yanks recently.

(Pause.)

OSCAR: OK, so you got fifteen poun's to throw away . . .

TONY: Right! So what I want you to do is put five on one horse an' ten on another - I got it all written -

OSCAR (on his feet): Hold it! You said *one* bet! Now you tellin' me about 'five on one horse, an' ten on another'. What you take me for, man? Ladbrokes!

TONY: Will you sit down, Oscar? Will you flickin' siddown.

(Pause.)

There's a fiver in this fo' you if I win.

OSCAR: Bribery?

TONY: Call it your commission.

OSCAR: Well, tha's diff'rent.

(Sits.)

I'm y'man.

TONY: Right! Now they're both fav'rites so they're pretty safe horses, but done play them as doubles or anyuh that, right, even fav'rites can lose, right?

OSCAR: OK, OK.

TONY: Good.

(Pause.)

Naturally they won't pay much being fav'rites. Accordin' to Mrs Frazier's paper (I ain' even had a chance to go out an' buy a mornin' *paper*) anyway accordin' to her Mirror they're givin' three to one odds on bothuh them. Which should bring about sixty poun's if they both come in.

OSCAR: Nice. How much you owe Rita?

TONY: I'm not finish yet. I got another horse fo' you.

OSCAR: Another horse! Jesus, I'll be in there all day. I'll have to carry san'wiches.

TONY: Done talk crap, man.

(Pause.)

A twenty-to-one horse; I want you to put the whole sixty on it.

OSCAR: The whole amount? A twenty-to-one horse! Tha's . . . six by two . . . tha's . . . that's . . . *over* a t'ousan' *poun's*.

(Pause.)

Plus y'sixty back. Lord, tha's *money*, boy.

TONY: One thousan', two hundred an' sixty poun's. Less tax of course.

OSCAR: I like it, I like it.

(Pause. Doubt.)

But a twenty-to-one horse?

TONY: This horse boun' an' oblige to win. When I say it boun' to win, I mean it *can't* lose! There ain' no way this horse can lose. No way, no way.

OSCAR: Who say so!

TONY: I say so! Me.

(Pause.)

Oscar I had m'eye on this filly since las' season! They breed it to run a mile, they breed this horse *special.* One *exact* mile. No more, no less. Right? An' that horse runnin' today in the four ten at Goodwood. An' guess what's the four ten at Goodwood today?

OSCAR: A mile?

TONY: You better believe it.

OSCAR: Money, I smell money!

TONY: Now you see why I want to put as much bread on that horse as I can get my han's on.

(Pause.)

OSCAR: An' what's the nameuh this horse?

TONY: Lady Laughter.

OSCAR (on his feet again): You *MAD*! Lady Laughter! You're an *ASS*, boy! That horse is so *lazy* my own daughter could run away from it!

TONY: That horse is a dead cert!

OSCAR: That horse is a dead duck! Sixty poun's on Lady Laughter! Fo' that kinduh money you done need to bet on it, you could *buy* it.

(Pause.)

TONY (his faith a bit shaken): You dunno what y'sayin', boy. My mind tell me to bet on this horse.

(OSCAR's laughter says exactly what he thinks of TONY's 'mind'.)

OK - OK, tell me what you got against it. If you know something I dunno, tell me. Done jus' stan' there laughin'.

OSCAR: Well fo' one thing, I know no self-respectin' jockey would even take it fo' a *walk*, much less ride it.

TONY: A concrete fact, Oscar! Give me one concrete fact against that horse.

OSCAR: It can't win: what more concrete fact you want than that?

(Pause.)

TONY: Oscar you're a blight. They oughta take you up to Heathrow airport an' put you on the nex' plane *outuh* here.

(Pause.)

OSCAR: I'm tryin' to save you money an' all the thanks I get is insults. If tha's not ingratitude, well, I dunno.

TONY: Oscar, I'm foamin' at the mouth, but I'm tryin' not to lose m'temper . . . !

OSCAR: OK, OK, buddy, if you won't take advice.

(Pause. Tony produces three fivers and a betting slip.)

TONY: Fifteen poun's, right? An' I got it all written out here. Right? The fav'rite in the two o'clock, the fav'rite in the three ten, an' then the full sixty poun's on Lady Laughter in the four ten. You got that?

OSCAR: Yeah, I got it. It's your funeral. Personally buddy, I wouldn't put a wreath on that horse much less sixty poun's.

TONY (a warning): Oscar, done mess me about.

(Pause. A cry.)

I got no choice, I owe it to Rita . . . !

OSCAR: OK, Tony, you know bes'.

TONY (moving towards the door): Well, look I gotta get back down there.

(At door.)

She's pretty sick really.

(He doesn't open the door.)

OSCAR: Tell her I'm sorry to hear that.

TONY (almost to himself): She seem to have real bad luck that girl.

(Pause.)

You reckon maybe I shouldn't do it . . . have this bet, I mean . . . when she's so sick, y'know?

(Pause.)

OSCAR (embarrassed): It's your wife, man, I couldn't answer that.

(Pause.)

TONY: We been waitin' an' waitin' fo' that ambulance. We could've walked there by now.

(Pause.)

If you ain' got money, not even the ambulance wants to know.

(He opens the door. They leave the room. Disappear down the passage. Pause.)

BLACKOUT

Scene Two

The FLETCHERS' room. Summer. Evening.

TONY comes bounding into the room, newspaper in hand. He has just learnt that all his horses have won. He switches on light in room.

TONY: Oh God, Oh God, boy . . . !

(Throws paper up in the air.)

Oh God, boy!

(OSCAR approaches his door. Knocks. TONY opens it with a flourish.)

Oscar! If you were a flag, I'd salute yuh!

OSCAR: Flag? What flag?

(TONY shuts the door. Rushes over to glass-top table.)

TONY: Put it right there! Right on top here.

(Wipes it with his hand.)

There, it's clean enough fo' any amountuh money.

OSCAR: You done want to sit down?

TONY: Thanks all the same, Oscar, but I live here, remember? Jus' forget y'*eti-ket* fo' once an' let's jus' see the colouruh the bread. Or maybe they give you a cheque, right?

OSCAR (not exactly happy): Cheque? No, no cheque.

TONY: Good, I'm not fussy.

(Pause.)

Well?

(Pause. OSCAR brings out some money. Lays out a hundred pounds in ten pound notes. Pause.)

TONY: What's that, Oscar? *Bus fare?*

(Pause.)

OSCAR: That's how much they gimme.

(Pause.)

TONY: What you mean 'tha's how much they gimme'! Even nurses make more money than that. Even *black* nurses.

OSCAR: Tha's a hundred poun's there, man. Good British money.

TONY: OK, so you're a patriotic black Englishman - now cut the foolin', where's ma money?

OSCAR: Tha's it.

TONY: What crap is this, Oscar?!

OSCAR: Will you jus' siddown, man, Tony.

TONY: I live here, Oscar!

(Pause.)

OSCAR: OK, so I'll siddown.

(Does so. Pause.)

TONY: Jesus Christ Almighty, if I had a dog, he'd be maulin' you right now. *I swear it.*

OSCAR: Will you let me explain, man, Tony!

TONY: OK, OK, I'm all ears.

(Silence from OSCAR.)

Speak up, Oscar, I can't hear you.

OSCAR: OK, OK, I bet the firs' two horses, y'know, the fav'rites . . .

TONY: An' what?

OSCAR: An' they won. Sixty poun's less tax, they pay me.

TONY: So then I tole you to put the full sixty on Lady Laughter to win, so what's the problem?

OSCAR (rising): I felt sure the horse had no chance.

TONY: I done believe it . . .

OSCAR: I only put two poun's fifty on the horse.

(Pause.)

TONY (he still can't believe it): You jokin'. You got to be jokin'. But I tole you . . . !

OSCAR: I know, I jus' din' think the horse could walk, never mind run.

(He doesn't like the way TONY is looking at him. He backs away.)

Man, I sorry bad.

(TONY has to sit on the bed.)

TONY: I coulda got a lunatic. I coulda stop by the nearest nuthouse an' got me a lunatic, an' everything woulda been fine. Instead I had to rely on a rass like you. All the mental hospitals in this country to choose from an' *look who I pick* . . . Judas. I pick Judas Escariot.

OSCAR: I did it fo' Rita. Fo' bothuh you.

TONY: I mean, that money woulda help to see me outuh here.

OSCAR: I wanted to make sure you at least had fifty poun's to pay back Rita.

TONY (a cry): That money woulda help see me outuh here . . . !

OSCAR: Tony, man, I'm sorry.

TONY: That money woulda help see me outuh here!

(And he suddenly erupts. He throws himself at OSCAR, and pins OSCAR's head in a hammer-lock, snarling and murderous as something from the forest.)

Murder yuh - I'll murder yuh!

OSCAR: Jesus - m'neck - Tony . . .

(The rest of his words degenerate into a series of strangled sounds. TONY seems bent on choking him to death. No one is playing games here.)

TONY: Shut it! Shut y'mouth!

(And draws back his fist as if he means to damage OSCAR's brain. But checks himself at the last moment. Pause. He releases OSCAR. OSCAR can hardly straighten up, not at first anyway. Pause. TONY tries to calm himself down.)

TONY: You lucky . . . ! I made a pact wit' m'self never to hit a fellow black man.

(Pause. He sits; worn down.)

That money was to help see me outuh here.

(Pause.)

She lost the baby, Oscar. M'wife jus' lost 'er baby. The doctors give 'er about three months to live.

(Pause.)

OSCAR (close to breaking point): I'd give m'right arm . . . m'arm. If it would help, I'd give m'right arm . . . !

(Pause.)

M'arm, Tony. I'd give m'right arm.

(Pause. TONY rises, goes to door, holds it open.)

Ow, Tony. I feel so bad. Done sen' me away like this, Tony.

(Pause.)

Tony.

(Pause. Abruptly.)

Everybody treats me like I'm garbage. White people - black people . . . ! I'm NOT GARBAGE . . . !

(Pause.)

I'm not garbage.

(Pause.)

I feel so bad.

(Pause.)

I'd give m'right arm.

(Pause. OSCAR shuffles out. Pause. TONY crosses over to the money; he seems to have no will, no volition left of his own. He brushes the money off the table with a disinterested flick of his fingers. Pause. His eyes rake the room: they reflect the weight of the room.)

TONY (a mumble): This room . . . this room.

(Pause. He throws himself down on top of the bed. Pause. A knock at his door. DENNIS. TONY sits up on the bed.)

Get lost! Or I swear, they'll give me a knighthood fo' murdering you . . . !

(DENNIS knocks again. TONY leaps at the door. Swings it open.)

Oh it's you, Dennis, sorry!

DENNIS: Peace.

(Both laugh loudly. DENNIS enters.)

TONY: I thought it was Oscar.

DENNIS: You thought I was Oscar ... !

(TONY suddenly realizes the money is still on the floor. DENNIS can hardly help noticing it, as well. TONY gets down on all fours to collect it.)

My God, Tony. You rob Barclay's Bank?

(Pause. No reply from TONY.)

Tony ... ?

(TONY slowly rises to one knee. Holds the money against his chest. He seems to be staring at something just out of reach. Then.)

TONY: It was supposed to be my insurance against white people. God had other ideas.

(Pause.)

Never misses a trick, does 'e?

(Pause. He gets to his feet. Puts money away in RITA's dressing table. DENNIS has found himself some place to sit.)

DENNIS: I come to enquire about Rita? How is she?

TONY: She loss the baby.

DENNIS: Oh no. Poor Rita.

TONY: Yeah, well, you can get used to anything.

DENNIS: How come you so hard, boy?

TONY (angry): You studying Sociology at that Poly-tec-nic. I work in a factory. Tha's how come.

(Pause. DENNIS takes off his glasses. Studies them. Pause.)

DENNIS (gravely): You make me sound like one o' them rich students. Onassis son-in-law. I work weekends, done forget. I'm not even a distant cousin of the King of Ethiopia.

TONY: I'm sorry, Dennis. It's just m'nerves talkin', man.

DENNIS: That summer job I've just finished .... You think that was a joke? Compared to that job your job is paradise. For a start there's no such thing as a union when you work at Morgan's Dress Hire shop. My job was to press the clothes after the customers brought them back; frock coats and dress suits and dinner-jackets smelling of wine and sweat. I mean most times that's all we did to them, iron the damn things. No nonsense about them being dry-cleaned first or anyuh that. Just a good pressing an' we pass them on to the next customer. You talk about the size of this room, that room was so small this room would swallow it. An' no windows. As God above me, no windows . . . ! A door to the shop, that's all. I use to iron with me shirt off. They din' call me Man Friday for nothing. An' to top it all they had a boiler in that room.

(He laughs.)

A boiler. Honest to God.

(Pause.)

I used to think I was going crazy. Heat . . . ! Jesus, boy. I never was that hot in Trinidad. Never.

(Pause.)

Yet, it's not the heat I remember most. It's the sweat. When that hot iron mixed with all that sweat something jus' had to give. Me, in the end.

BLACKOUT.

Scene Three

House in Shepherd's Bush. The FLETCHERS' room.

RITA is sitting propped up on the settee. TONY has bought a number of flowers in honour of her return. He has only been able to locate one vase so he has had to resort to a number of milk bottles. He still has not completed the stereo set. He has however built the amplifier now. The television set he has been repairing is gone. DENNIS is having coffee with them. A bottle of Lucozade and a glass on glass-top table.

TONY: I never heard nothing so crazy in m'whole life!

RITA (great sigh): Try not to shout, Tony.

(Pause.)

I need a holiday an' I want to see Binkie. An' that's that. How much those flowers coss you? An' why milk bottles, if you done mine me askin'? Why milk bottles?

TONY: Done knock them, they're genuine antiques. From United Dairies.

(RITA turns away, bored by him. Pause.)

You sure you won't prefer to be in bed, girl?

RITA (a sigh): What? What's this now? Bed? What for? I'm comfortable enough here.

(Short pause.)

TONY (quiet, sad): Suit y'self.

(Pause. Abruptly.)

You mean to go even if it kill you!

RITA: You sure you're sane, boy?

(Pause. TONY stalks over to the bed. Starts changing his shoes.)

DENNIS: Am, I think what Tony means Rita, is that, well, you're not exactly in the bestuh health, girl, an' Trinidad is so far away.

RITA: Dennis, the doctor let me outuh hospital because I really need a holiday, Dennis.

(Pause. Both men look down at the floor. Pause.)

Well, ain' that true?

(Pause.)

I haven't seen Binkie in months, Dennis.

(Pause.)

A woman's chil'ren are important to her. Men done understan' jus' how important.

(Pause.)

I jus' lost a baby. I need to be wit' Binkie. Fo' *my* own good.

(Pause.)

No man can understan' what an abortion or a miscarriage can do to a woman. The effect it can have on 'er.

(Pause.)

TONY: I understan' all that - but you can still wait an' see how things go. Insteaduh rushin' off like Speedy Gonzales.

(A cry.)

I mean suppose something was to happen to you, Rita! F'Godsakes Rita, done do this to me . . . !

(Pause. DENNIS embarrassed.)

DENNIS: I think I'd better split, leave you two to be alone.

RITA: Done talk rot, Dennis. Stay an' have some more coffee.

DENNIS: No. Thanks.

(Yawning.)

Gotta be off.

(Then.)

Tell you what, if you get y'ticket an' things fixed up in time fo' Tuesday an' if you haven't changed y'mind by then, I'll give you a lift to the airport. Gimme a ring, OK?

RITA: You're an angel, Dennis.

TONY: Boy, whose side're you on, eh?

(DENNIS laughs ruefully.)

DENNIS: See you, Rita. Take care.

RITA: Bye Dennis.

(DENNIS leaves the room. Steps into passage. TONY follows. Closes door behind him. RITA turns her head away. She falls into an abstracted state.)

DENNIS: You got to tell her, man!

TONY: Keep y'voice down, Chrise.

DENNIS: You got to tell her.

TONY: You tell 'er, nuh. Go ahead.

(Pause.)

DENNIS: I know it's hard man, Tony, but you got no choice.

(Pause.)

TONY (not looking at DENNIS): Boy, I dunno what to do . . . I jus' dunno what to do.

(Pause.)

Chrise, man, Chrise.

(Pause.)

DENNIS: Maybe the doctor, y'know, maybe he made a mistake. Half the time doctors dunno what they're doing.

TONY: A mistake . . . ! Wit' her luck. God hates us both too much fo' that.

(Pause.)

DENNIS (blurting it out): You should at least go with her!

TONY: To Trinidad. You know how much it costs, there and back. Eh? It's not the same as a day trip to Sout'end, sport.

DENNIS: OK, OK. Then tell her an' get it over with. I'm sure she wouldn't go anywhere if she knew.

TONY (almost too disgruntled to laugh): Boy, you dunno Rita. My wife is so stubborn mules queue up fo' her autograph. The only reason she never won a price fo' stubbornness is because she's too stubborn to compete wit' other people.

DENNIS: Boy, you're too much. Be seeing you, man, Tony.

TONY: See yuh.

(DENNIS goes. TONY returns inside. RITA is still just sitting there looking abstracted.)

TONY (a bit unsure of her reaction): You OK, honey?

(No reaction. Pause.)

Why take things out on me, Rita?

(Pause.)

RITA: You got this place in a state again.

(Pause.)

What'd you do when I'm not here? Entertain all those jockeys that never win a race fo' you?

(Pause.)

An' do they always have to bring their horses along as well?

(Pause.)

TONY (loudly): You're not goin' on any trip an' that's final!

(Pause.)

RITA (unperturbed): I got to go, Tony.

TONY: Over m'dead body.

RITA: Done tempt me, boy.

(They look at each other. Pause.)

Maybe you care to tell me this, how you expec' the chile to come back if I done go fo' him? You plan to hire a nanny, perhaps?

TONY: He can come back the same way he went.

RITA: Wit' Mrs Gomes. Y'jokin' or what? She won't be back till December. You think I could live wit'out m'son fo' that long. What kinduh parent are you?

(Pause.)

TONY: Why not write y'mother an' ask 'er to bring him 'ome. Write an' invite 'er fo' a holiday.

(Pause.)

I done mine 'er stayin' a day or so.

(Pause.)

We can always sen' 'er out to work if she stay longer. They always need traffic wardens so she won't have to worry.

(Pause.)

She could even bring y'father if she done mine walkin' wit' him. A bit difficult findin' him a job, though. Not much work about these days fo' a pensioner who flatly refuses to leave his wheelchair.

(He laughs boyishly.)

Lead me to the Palladium, I'm wasted here.

RITA: Tell me when y'finish *ramblin' on an'* I'll lead you to the *cemetery*. You'd really *waste* away there.

(Pause.)

TONY: I done fine anyuh this amusin' *neither*, believe me. None of it need ever'uve happened if you hadn' disobeyed me in the firse place!

RITA: Disobeyed you! Since when yo' m'father?

TONY: I still can't comprehend it . . . ! The way your mine works! Why'd you go through wit' it?! What sortuh loser are you, girl!

RITA (a yawn, then): I done even know what yuh talkin' about.

TONY: The chile. That's what! The chile!

(Pause.)

You knew the danger - Jesus, Jesus, the doctor spelled it out fo' you - *no more children* - yet you went right ahead an' got y'self pregnant.

RITA: I can't believe it . . . ! My name is not the Virgin Mary. I had some help, done forget that.

(For a moment or two TONY seems stuck for words. Then.)

TONY: You were fitted wit' a coil. A coil. It's supposed to be *at least* as effective as a chastity belt.

RITA: The maternity hospital's fulluh women who put their trust in the coil.

TONY (low): Then women must be more stupid than they look.

RITA (dagger-sharp): I beg y'pardon?

TONY: Nothing. I never said a word.

(Pause.)

Anyway, the point is you wanted the chile, you were *determined* to have it. That's the point. You wouldn't even *hear* about an abortion. Chrise man, Chrise. Wit' your medical history you coulda had an abortion as easy as fallin' down the stairs.

RITA (loudly): *Shut up.*

(Pause. She gets up. Pours herself some Lucozade. Sits down again.)

TONY (sad): It's y'mentality. I done mean to hurt you honey, God knows, but it's y'mentality, that's what bothers me. Ow, Rita, you coulda died. You coulda died. You knew that, yet there was no gettin' through to you.

(Pause.)

All these months all this expense, girl, it need nevera happened, Rita. *Do you comprehend what I'm sayin'?* All that's happened these las' months - Binkie havin' to go home, the hospital, everything - none of it need ever'uve happened!

(Pause. A cry.)

Rita, I've had to pay fo' *your* stubborness . . . !

(Pause.)

RITA (a stranger): Leave me then. Go on. Why done you leave me, eh? If that's the way you feel. Jus' go. Bye, bye.

TONY (quietly): Done say that, Rita.

RITA (losing control): Leave me be! I wish to Christ you would jus' clear outah m'sight! You're always underfoot, *Jesus*.

(Pause.)

All fo' nothing . . . after four ripe months . . . an' now you come telling me about my mentality. Who the hell you think you are?

(Ugly.)

You can't make up fo' what I lost: you want it any more plain than that?

(Pause. Sad, trying to be less unkind.)

You are not enough . . . not any more, daddy.

(Pause. TONY leaves the room, blindly. Pause.)

Scene Four

The FLETCHERS' room. Night. TONY and RITA in bed. Darkness.

TONY: Rita.

(Pause.)

Rita.

(Pause.)

Rita . . . !

RITA: Boy, I'm trying to sleep.

(Pause.)

TONY: Are you OK?

RITA (not particularly positive about it): I'm OK.

(Pause.)

TONY: I'll get y'medicine if it'll help you feel better.

RITA: I said I'm OK, give it a rest.

(Pause.)

TONY: I almos' finished the set. The stereo. You want to see it?

RITA: At two o'clock in the morning . . . !

(Pause.)

Not even Lassie should be awake at this hour.

TONY: I know, you feelin' bad, but Christ . . . !

RITA: Now where you off to?

(Pause. Apparently he has got out of bed. Pause. The room is still in complete darkness.)

TONY: Rita, what's gone wrong wit' us? What 'ave I done wrong, girl?

RITA: Boy, we have to discuss this now? Eh?

(Pause.)

TONY: I can't get through to you. This is no time fo' a . . . *wall* between us.

(Pause.)

Done lock me out, Rita.

(Pause.)

Please, please.

(Pause.)

Please, Rita.

(Pause.)

What've I done wrong, girl?

(A cry.)

Rita, ah'm fightin' fo' m'life, Rita!

(Pause.)

RITA: I can't be consoled . . . I refuse to be consoled.

(Pause.)

Scene Five

The FLETCHERS' room. Day.

TONY alone in the room. At his work-bench. Soldering iron in hand repairing a transistor radio. He is wearing a matching shirt and tie, grey trousers; he is dressed to go with RITA to the airport. He has finally finished building the stereo set. The complete set is laid out on the floor and covered over by a dust sheet.

Two suitcases, one larger than the other, packed and ready for RITA's departure. The door opens: RITA. She remains in doorway. She does not seem very well. She has bought a pair of shoes.

TONY (rising): Are you mad, girl? Eh? Dennis will soon be here, you forget.

(Pause. He goes to her.)

Girl, you look like hell!

RITA: I'm OK.

(But she has to hold on to him. Pause.)

TONY: It start again?

RITA: I'm OK, I said.

(Pause.)

TONY (a cry): Why'd you go out!

RITA (wan smile): In a few hours I plan to cross a mighty ocean, I should at lease be able to cross the street by m'self.

(Pause. TONY helps her towards the settee. She spies covered-up stereo set.)

What's that, Tony - a shroud? Who y'got under there - Vincent Price?

(She sits gingerly. TONY moves away trying to find her medicine.)

TONY: Where's y'medicine?

RITA: You finally finish it, the set? What you hidin' it for?

(He gives her two of her tablets. With some Lucozade to wash them down. Pause.)

RITA (looking down at the floor, more to herself than to him): I nearly died the las' time.

(Pause. Still not looking at him.)

Did they tell you that?

(Pause.)

One more time like that an' they can sen' fo' the hearse an' the flowers . . . an' the man in the black suit who keeps his han's behin' his back.

(Pause.)

TONY: You pack everything?

RITA: What? Nat'rally. Excep' fo' those shoes. That's how come I went out, I needed new shoes. You want m'mother to think you can't afford to buy me a proper pairuh shoes. You want 'er to think I'm married to a black Scotsman.

(TONY's reaction is to suck his teeth.)

How about you, you ready?

TONY: Sure, I'm only goin' to the airport. I won't be gettin' on the plane, so you done have to worry about that.

RITA: What're you gettin' at now?

(And looks away: it's all such a drag. Pause.)

TONY (crying out): You can't even bear my company any more . . . ! It's *obvious*. I'm not a complete ass!

(Pause.)

Firse you're away fo' three months, then fo' nearly two weeks, an' now when you're finally home, what d'you do? You jump on the first plane to Trinidad! Obvious! I'm not a complete ass. A holiday trip, you call it. I call it grounds fo' divorce!

(Pause. Plaintive.)

Other women put their men firse. The way you treat me anyone would think you married the Hunchback o' Notre Dame.

(Pause.)

You'd rather go in hospital than be wit' me.

(Pause. A cry.)

If I was to get on that plane wit' you, you'd pay them to hi-jack it.

(Pause. He stands before her, worn down.)

RITA: Boy, I'm feelin' drained . . . y'understan', *drained* . . . too drained to go through a vaudeville act wit' you. OK?

(Pause.)

TONY (nakedly): These days you never have time fo' me, Rita . . . !

(Pause. Hardly a joke as far as he is concerned.)

You're never aroun' when I need you. Even Count Dracula stays home in the daytime.

(Pause.)

RITA: I've been sick, in case you haven't noticed.

(Pause.)

TONY: Even before you got sick you never had much time fo' me.

RITA: Done talk rot, boy.

(Pause.)

TONY: Many's the time I try to touch your skin, an' I watch you draw away . . . like I had leprosy or something.

RITA: Rubbish.

(Pause.)

Sheer rubbish.

(Pause.)

Anyway I done go wit' other men, that's all that matters.

TONY (a cry): That's not enough . . . ! I need joy too, an', an' *warmth,*
man. A woman who's faithful but cold jus' faithful alone, but without
juice or - *joy* - oh God, such a woman is like ah marble egg: perfec'
outside, a perfec' shape, but you can't get no nourishment from it.

(Pause.)

Well, say something, Rita.

(Pause.)

Rita, I'm so sickuh m'own company you got no idea.

(Pause. Anything to get through to her.)

I know it's not nice to say, but I want a companion not a hospital
patient!

(Pause.)

RITA: Thanks. Thanks a lot.

(Pause.)

TONY: I haven't been happy fo' months - years - an' you done even know
it! I AM A HUNDRED PERCENT DISSATISFIED WIT' OUR
MARRIAGE! God, Rita.

(Pause.)

Things used to be so diff'rent. Coulda been diff'rent.

(Pause.)

You done seem to be able to give me what I need any more.

(Pause.)

Either you're never there or when you're there you're ambulance
material.

(Ugly.)

Either way you're useless to me. Useless, useless!

(Pause.)

RITA (leaving settee): Boy, you're a bastard an' a half.

(She helps herself to more Lucozade.)

TONY (wearily): I am a hundred percent dissatisfied wit' our marriage.

(Pause.)

This room . . . this room.

(Pause.)

RITA (sitting down again): OK, let's talk about this room shall we? You
always goin' on about this room, well let's talk about it Mr Smartass.

TONY (a threat): Watch y'step, woman.

(Pause.)

RITA: Is this the bes' we can do? As a chargehan' you make enough, not a pile, not too much, but you done do too badly, so how come this one room? Can't we do better? Eh?

TONY: Our Lord started out in a manger . . . !

RITA: An' look where he ended up, on a *cross*.

(Pause.)

Comeon, let's have it out.

TONY (walking away, low growl): You can't be sick in truth.

RITA: Come back here. Hide is the one thing you can't do in here.

(Then.)

We're always talkin' about y'gamblin', right? But what we never get down to is how *long* you been gamblin'. Right?

(Pause.)

You been gamblin' fo' so long even the horses should club together an' buy you a gold watch.

TONY: Joke. Big joke. Ask y'self this question, would I spen' so much time in the bettin' shop if I was gettin' the right odds at home?

(Pause.)

RITA: All I know is how much money you lost. Y'thrown away at least a fiver every week - fo' years now.

TONY (holding his head in his hands): I'm talkin' about our marriage - God knows any way you look at it we got about as much future as the Titanic - yet this girl got nothing else on her mine but money.

(Pause.)

RITA: Five poun's, sometimes ten poun's. Its madness!

TONY: What're yuh talkin' about? Every week who loses ten poun's . . . ! You're talkin' to a professional. A professional.

(In spite of himself.)

Not Donald Duck.

RITA: You make me sick.

(Pause.)

I could throw up. Jus' throw up.

(Pause.)

Five, ten poun's, time after time. You're lucky you're married to me, damn lucky. Most other women woulda been off by now. They wouldn't even bother to wake yuh up to say goodbye.

(Pause.)

TONY (almost to himself): Women, boy. They never try fo' a knockout. They jus' cut yuh up. Scientifically.

(Pause.)

After that the only hope you got is that the ref might take pity on you . . . an' stop the fight in time.

RITA: What yuh mumblin' about?

(Then.)

You know how much you threw away las' year? I figured it out Mr *Sportsman.* Know how much? Eh?

(Pause.)

Something like three hundred poun's. Three hundred poun's, Tony. Oh Lord.

(Pause.)

To some white people three hundred poun's is nothing but to people like us it's the diff'rence between a proper place to live an' being stuck here like Bostik!

(Pause.)

You never stop goin' on about the house we could buy if you were a big-shot accountant: try thinkin' about the nice flat we could be in right now if you weren't such a big-shot *gambler.*

(Pause.)

What sortuh man would dump his wife in one room like this . . . . Call y'self a man? Call y'self a man?

(Pause.)

TONY: An' you're supposed to be sick. Boy, it's good a thing you're not alive an' well, or I'd be done for.

(Then.)

Who'm I tryin' to kid? I'm done for now. The nex' time that guy comes by shoutin' fo' scrap-iron, I'll jus' throw myself on 'is cart an' 'is mercy.

(Pause.)

RITA (she can afford a little mercy now): Jus' can't take it, can you?

(Pause.)

You take me too seriously, Tony.

(Pause.)

Comeon, I got a bit angry, so what?

(Pause.)

Boy, you take me so seriously.

(Pause.)

Comeon, show me that set you got buried under that *shroud*.

(Pause. Neither moves. Loss.)

These days I ain' exactly good value m'self, am I?

(Pause.)

I talk about you, what kinduh wife am I? I can't even let you make love to me.

(Weary laugh. Pause.)

TONY: Yeah, well, this ain' exactly the bes' time to worry about that.

(Pause.)

RITA (sagging, for the first time): No, I suppose not.

(Pause. Her head down.)

When I come back . . . if that's what you want. . .

TONY: I can't hear a word.

(Pause.)

RITA: Come 'ere.

(Pause. He goes to her. She touches his hand.)

I said when I return you can divorce me . . . if that's what you want.

TONY (moving away): What y'talkin' about . . .

(A cry.)

Jus' how sick do you have to be before you wake up to how sick you really are . . . !

(Pause.)

RITA: That sounds like double dutch to me.

(Pause.)

TONY: Use y'head fo' once in y'life. Doctors done let their patients out to visit their relatives without havin' some good, good reason. They're not in the travel business, woman!

(Pause.)

RITA: What you tryin' to say, boy?

(Pause.)

TONY: I'm no doctor. I got nothing to say.

(Pause.)

RITA: It'll do me good, Tony. A holiday, goin' home, walkin' down Henry Street, seein' Binkie again, seein' m'chile again, it'll do me good . . . . Boun' to do me good.

TONY: Jesus, Jesus.

    (He has to sit down. He hides his head in his hands. Pause.)

RITA: We gotta keep believin', Tony, or we'll never make it.

    (Pause.)

    What's the matter?

    (He straightens up.)

TONY: Nothing.

    (Pause.)

RITA: I'll be back in a month's time. One month.

TONY: Yeah, sure.

    (Pause.)

RITA: Tell you what would be nice, if on m'way back I could perhaps visit Guyana.

    (Pause.)

TONY (trying to focus): Eh . . . ? Eh . . . ? Guyana?

RITA: Sure, why not? A wife should visit her husband's birt'place at lease once in 'er life.

    (Pause.)

    Tell me about the seawall.

    (She flinches.)

TONY: You OK?

RITA: I'm OK. I feel a bit . . .

    (Pause.)

    I'll be OK.

    (Pause.)

    Tell me about the seawall.

TONY: The seawall?

RITA: The Georgetown seawall, silly. You use to tell me about it. Tell me again, daddy.

TONY: Why the seawall . . . ! It keeps the sea out, like any other seawall. You see one, you seen 'em all.

    (Pause.)

    Funny, I done even think about it anymore.

    (Pause.)

    It use to be a great place to take a chick at night. I mean if a chick allowed you to take 'er out on the seawall after nine at night, it was a pretty safe bet she'd let you in by half pas' nine!

(Pause.)

But it was in the afternoon, that's when you'd fine the most people out on the seawall. Aroun' six o'clock, it use to be like a promenade out there. A parade. Everybody would turn up on their bicycles. The girls firse, they'd park their bikes an' sit out on the wall an' wait for the boys, they'd wear their prettiest frocks. You'd see them all the way along the wall, birds on a fence . . . black chicks, brown chicks, Chinese, Indian, even one or two white chicks, all waitin' to see an' be seen. An' then the guys would arrive, some wit' sunglasses on, an' some wit' han'ker-chiefs tied roun' their necks. I mean those guys use to look pretty sharp, you know what I mean, Loopy Loo . . . ! They were pretty sharp guys an' they'd ride up an' down, up an' down in frontuh the girls, tryin' to chat them up, tryin' to pull a chick fo' Saturday night. But the girls would stay cool. They'd stay cool an' laugh among them-selves an' play hard to get, the way girls do the worl' over.

(Pause.)

Later aroun' seven o'clock we'd all get back on our bikes an' head fo' home, makin' plans to meet again the followin' night, same time, same place.

(Pause. Wearily.)

I use to be so young, Loopy Loo.

(Pause.)

I knew nex' to nothing about white people.

(Almost in spite of himself.)

That's the kinduh ignorance that's real bliss, Loopy Loo.

(Pause.)

I use to be so young, girl, now I back horses that boun' an' 'blige to win, only how come they never do?

(Pause.)

How many years you reckon we got to live in this country before they stop callin' us immigrants?

(Pause.)

Eh, Loopy Loo? How many years?

RITA: Tony, there's something I been meanin' to ask you fo' some time now . . . done be angry but, I wish you won't call me Loopy Loo no more, Tony.

(Pause.)

TONY (involuntary): God, oh God.

(He squats down beside her, hugging her awkwardly, fiercely.)

Done go, Rita . . . ! Ow Rita.

RITA: Y'hurtin' me.

(She holds him off. Pause. Struggles to her feet.)

I gotta go. Be sensible, there's no two ways about it.

(Pause.)

TONY (straightening up): Go then. *Bitch.* I hope to Chrise the worse happen! Look at you. Jus' look at you. You can hardly stan' up! M'gamblin'! You talk about m'gamblin'! You must be jokin'.

(Pause.)

When is the las' time you ever enjoyed anything? Work, cook, sleep, get up, work, hospital, more work, more hospital. That's not life, what you live, that's jus' God havin' a joke at your expense.

(Pause.)

You got any *idea* of the diff'rence between your life an' a middle-class white woman's life? Eh? Y'got any idea?

(Pause.)

What've you got to show fo' twenty-five years?

(Pause.)

You're all the proof I need, girl. At lease I got the horses. You done even take a drink once in a while. You gotta have something to help you stay afloat . . . ! I'm not talkin' about excess, but Jesus, we deserve some sortuh compensation. Surely.

(Pause. She is putting the shoes in her suitcase.)

The one thing we got any right to in this life is to *enjoy*. Surely.

(Pause. Sad.)

Someone must know.

(Pause.)

Well, say something, nuh!

(She continues to fuss over her suitcase. Pause.)

RITA: Dennis should be here soon.

(Pause.)

TONY: You understan' nothing. Noneuh you.

(Pause.)

Everybody think they g'un live fo'ever.

RITA (finally treating him to her opinion): Throwin' y'money away in a bettin' shop. That's your idea of enjoyin' y'self.

(She sucks her teeth.)

We'll never make it, eh boy? West Indian men.

(Pause. She crosses to the covered-up set.)

Can I see y'set now?

(Pause.)

Come on. Or are you gettin' the queen to unveil it?

TONY (almost in spite of himself): I was thinkin' of gettin' one of y'relations. Y'half mad uncle, perhaps. The one who sleepwalks so much at night he's got to take a map to bed wit' 'im to help him fine his way back in the morning.

(Pause.)

I'll even provide a fancy ribbon fo' 'im to cut when the time comes. Wit' any luck he might get so carried away he might cut his own throat as well.

RITA: Boy, why you done appear on Tee Vee? We could turn y'off then.

(She unveils the set. Turntable, amplifier, two large loudspeakers.)

Oh Tony, it's *beau - ti -ful.*

(Pause.)

Boy, what you want wit' any bettin' shop when you can build something like this? Eh?

(Pause.)

Put a record on.

(Pause.)

Once you can build something like this the odds are in our favour, Tony.

(He puts on a record. Pause.)

TONY: Not a bad sound at all, even if I say so m'self.

(DENNIS arrives in hallway. Knocks. TONY turns set off. Pause.)

RITA: You make me feel proud, proud, Tony.

(Pause.)

TONY (wry): Yeah, well, better late than never.

(Pause. She takes his hands in hers. Touches her lips to them. DENNIS knocks again.)

TONY (not looking away from RITA): It's open, Dennis.

(DENNIS enters.)

DENNIS: What's up? Y'ready?

RITA (not looking away from TONY): Come in, Dennis, I'm all ready.

(Then.)

Keep at it, Tony. The odds can only get better.

(Pause. TONY puts on his jacket. RITA has kept her coat on throughout this scene. DENNIS takes larger suitcase. TONY takes smaller one. He moves to help RITA. She prefers to walk with as little help as possible. All three leave the room.)

END OF PLAY

OTHER METHUEN PLAYSCRIPTS

Paul Ableman	TESTS
	BLUE COMEDY
Andrei Amalrik	EAST-WEST and IS UNCLE JACK
	A CONFORMIST?
Ed Berman/Justin Wintle	THE FUN ART BUS
Barry Bermange	NATHAN AND TABILETH AND
	OLDENBERG
John Bowen	THE CORSICAN BROTHERS
Howard Brenton	REVENGE
	CHRISTIE IN LOVE and OTHER PLAYS
	PLAYS FOR PUBLIC PLACES
	MAGNIFICENCE
Henry Chapman	YOU WON'T ALWAYS BE ON TOP
Peter Cheeseman (Ed)	THE KNOTTY
Caryl Churchill	OWNERS
David Cregan	THREE MEN FOR COLVERTON
	TRANSCENDING and THE DANCERS
	THE HOUSES BY THE GREEN
	MINIATURES
	THE LAND OF PALMS and
	OTHER PLAYS
Alan Cullen	THE STIRRINGS IN SHEFFIELD ON
	A SATURDAY NIGHT
Rosalyn Drexler	THE INVESTIGATION and
	HOT BUTTERED ROLL
Simon Gray	THE IDIOT
Henry Livings	GOOD GRIEF!
	THE LITTLE MRS FOSTER SHOW
	HONOUR AND OFFER
	PONGO PLAYS 1-6
	THIS JOCKY DRIVES LATE NIGHTS
	THE FFINEST FFAMILY IN THE LAND
John McGrath	EVENTS WHILE GUARDING THE
	BOFORS GUN
David Mercer	THE GOVERNOR'S LADY
Georges Michel	THE SUNDAY WALK
Rodney Milgate	A REFINED LOOK AT EXISTENCE
Guillaume Oyono-Mbia	THREE SUITORS: ONE HUSBAND and
	UNTIL FURTHER NOTICE
Alan Plater	CLOSE THE COALHOUSE DOOR
David Selbourne	THE PLAY OF WILLIAM COOPER AND
	EDMUND DEW-NEVETT
	THE TWO-BACKED BEAST
	DORABELLA
Wole Soyinka	CAMWOOD ON THE LEAVES

Johnny Speight	IF THERE WEREN'T ANY BLACKS YOU'D HAVE TO INVENT THEM
Martin Sperr	TALES FROM LANDSHUT
Boris Vian	THE KNACKER'S ABC
Lanford Wilson	HOME FREE! and THE MADNESS OF LADY BRIGHT
Harrison, Melfi, Howard	NEW SHORT PLAYS
Duffy, Harrison, Owens	NEW SHORT PLAYS: 2
Barker, Grillo, Haworth, Simmons	NEW SHORT PLAYS: 3

METHUEN'S MODERN PLAYS

Edited by John Cullen and Geoffrey Strachan

Paul Ableman	GREEN JULIA
Jean Anouilh	ANTIGONE
	BECKET
	POOR BITOS
	RING ROUND THE MOON
	THE LARK
	THE REHEARSAL
	THE FIGHTING COCK
	DEAR ANTOINE
	THE DIRECTOR OF THE OPERA
John Arden	SERJEANT MUSGRAVE'S DANCE
	THE WORKHOUSE DONKEY
	ARMSTRONG'S LAST GOODNIGHT
	LEFT-HANDED LIBERTY
	SOLIDER, SOLDIER AND OTHER PLAYS
	TWO AUTOBIOGRAPHICAL PLAYS
John Arden and	THE BUSINESS OF GOOD GOVERNMENT
Margaretta D'Arcy	THE ROYAL PARDON
	THE HERO RISES UP
Ayckbourn, Bowen, Brook, Campton, Melly, Owen, Pinter, Saunders, Weldon	MIXED DOUBLES
Brendan Behan	THE QUARE FELLOW
	THE HOSTAGE
	RICHARD'S CORK LEG
Barry Bermange	NO QUARTER AND THE INTERVIEW
Edward Bond	SAVED
	NARROW ROAD TO THE DEEP NORTH
	THE POPE'S WEDDING

	LEAR
	THE SEA
John Bowen	LITTLE BOXES
	THE DISORDERLY WOMEN
Bertolt Brecht	MOTHER COURAGE
	THE CAUCASIAN CHALK CIRCLE
	THE GOOD PERSON OF SZECHWAN
	THE LIFE OF GALILEO
	THE THREEPENNY OPERA
Syd Cheatle	STRAIGHT UP
Shelagh Delaney	A TASTE OF HONEY
	THE LION IN LOVE
Max Frisch	THE FIRE RAISERS
	ANDORRA
Jean Giraudoux	TIGER AT THE GATES
Simon Gray	SPOILED
	BUTLEY
Peter Handke	OFFENDING THE AUDIENCE and
	SELF-ACCUSATION
	KASPAR
	THE RIDE ACROSS LAKE CONSTANCE
Rolf Hochhuth	THE REPRESENTATIVE
Heinar Kipphardt	IN THE MATTER OF J. ROBERT
	OPPENHEIMER
Arthur Kopit	CHAMBER MUSIC and OTHER PLAYS
	INDIANS
Jakov Lind	THE SILVER FOXES ARE DEAD
	and OTHER PLAYS
David Mercer	ON THE EVE OF PUBLICATION
	AFTER HAGGERTY
	FLINT
John Mortimer	THE JUDGE
	FIVE PLAYS
	COME AS YOU ARE
	A VOYAGE ROUND MY FATHER
	COLLABORATORS
Joe Orton	CRIMES OF PASSION
	LOOT
	WHAT THE BUTLER SAW
	FUNERAL GAMES and
	THE GOOD AND FAITHFUL SERVANT
	ENTERTAINING MR SLOANE
Harold Pinter	THE BIRTHDAY PARTY
	THE ROOM and THE DUMB WAITER
	THE CARETAKER
	A SLIGHT ACHE and OTHER PLAYS
	THE COLLECTION and THE LOVER

	THE HOMECOMING
	TEA PARTY and OTHER PLAYS
	LANDSCAPE AND SILENCE
	OLD TIMES
David Selbourne	THE DAMNED
Jean-Paul Sartre	CRIME PASSIONNEL
Wole Soyinka	MADMEN AND SPECIALISTS
	THE JERO PLAYS
Boris Vian	THE EMPIRE BUILDERS
Peter Weiss	TROTSKY IN EXILE
Theatre Workshop	OH WHAT A LOVELY WAR
and Charles Chilton	
Charles Wood	'H'
	VETERANS
Carl Zuckmayer	THE CAPTAIN OF KOPENICK

METHUEN'S THEATRE CLASSICS

THE TROJAN WOMEN	Euripides
	an English version by Neil Curry
THE BACCHAE OF	an English version by Wole Soyinka
EURIPIDES	
THE REDEMPTION	Molière
	translated by Richard Wilbur
LADY PRECIOUS STREAM	adapted by S. I. Hsiung from a sequence
	of traditional Chinese plays
IRONHAND	Goethe
	adapted by John Arden
THE GOVERNMENT	Gogol
INSPECTOR	an English version by Edward O. Marsh
	and Jeremy Brooks
DANTON'S DEATH	Buechner
	an English version by James Maxwell
LONDON ASSURANCE	Boucicault
	adapted and edited by Ronald Eyre
BRAND	Ibsen
HEDDA GABLER	translated by Michael Meyer
THE WILD DUCK	
THE MASTER BUILDER	
GHOSTS	
PEER GYNT	
A DOLL'S HOUSE	
AN ENEMY OF THE PEOPLE	

MISS JULIE	Strindberg translated by Michael Meyer
THE IMPORTANCE OF BEING EARNEST LADY WINDERMERE'S FAN	Wilde
THE UBU PLAYS	Jarry translated by Cyril Connolly and Simon Watson Taylor
ENEMIES	Gorky
THE LOWER DEPTHS	English versions by Kitty Hunter-Blair and Jeremy Brooks
THE PLAYBOY OF THE WESTERN WORLD	Synge

If you would like regular information
on new Methuen plays, please write to
The Marketing Department
Eyre Methuen Ltd
11 New Fetter Lane
London EC4P 4EE